THE GOOD COUP

THE OVERTHROW OF MANUEL ZELAYA IN HONDURAS

MARCO CÁCERES DI IORIO

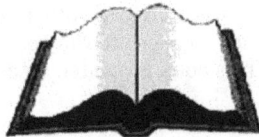

CCB Publishing
British Columbia, Canada

The Good Coup: The Overthrow of Manuel Zelaya in Honduras

ISBN-13 978-1-926918-07-5
First Edition

Library and Archives Canada Cataloguing in Publication
Cáceres di Iorio, Marco, 1958-
The good coup : the overthrow of Manuel Zelaya in Honduras / written by
Marco Cáceres di Iorio – 1st ed.
ISBN 978-1-926918-07-5
1. Honduras--History--Coup d'état, 2009.
2. Zelaya, Manuel, 1952-. 3. Honduras--Politics and government--1982-.
4. Honduras--History--1982-. I. Title.
F1508.3.C32 2010   972.8305'3   C2010-905485-7

Cover artwork: The image of the painting "El Mago" (The Magician) for the
front cover of this book is used with permission from Honduran artist Felipe
Burchard.

Extreme care has been taken to ensure that all information presented in this
book is accurate and up to date at the time of publishing. Neither the author
nor the publisher can be held responsible for any errors or omissions.
Additionally, neither is any liability assumed for damages resulting from the
use of the information contained herein.

Publisher: CCB Publishing
              British Columbia, Canada
              www.ccbpublishing.com

To my parents, who have always reminded me of my Honduran roots and helped fuel my passion for Honduras through family, travel, infinite stories, and an indefinable energy that inspires me to feel a special warmth toward my native land.

CONTENTS

PREFACE

I thought long and hard about the title of this book. I chose "The Good Coup" knowing full well that it would please no one and probably anger some. On the one hand, those who believe that the overthrow of Manuel "Mel" Zelaya as president of Honduras on June 28, 2009 was a military coup d'état, or *golpe de estado* (or more literally, a "hit job on the state") will no doubt take issue with my characterization of what occurred as "good". On the other hand, those who believe Mr. Zelaya's overthrow was a "constitutional transition of power" will take exception to my use of the word "coup". While the former assumes that all coups are inherently bad because they involve the forceful removal of a sitting president (and in this case, one who was democratically elected), the latter assumes that using the word coup automatically delegitimizes what occurred. I hold a different view.

As a rule, I believe coups are a bad thing, just as war is a bad thing. Both should be avoided and discouraged because they usually involve killing people – often, innocent people – and the destruction of property and disruption of public order, civility. They leave societies traumatized and turn back the clock on their development. Yet, most people would agree that there is such a thing as a "just war" – that sometimes situations become so threatening and unbearable that the use of force is the only effective response left.

I apply this same logic to coups. If you can have a "good war", then why can't you have a "good coup"? Certainly, wars are infinitely worse than coups. They last longer. They kill more people. And they are murkier from a legal standpoint because they usually involve two or more sovereign nations and the violation of geographic borders.

Unfortunately, too much of the debate about Mr. Zelaya's overthrow has been dominated by the questions of whether the action was a coup or not a coup, and whether it was constitutional or not constitutional. Obviously, these are important questions. The problem is that there does not appear to be a clearly right or wrong answer. Those on each side of the argument make valid points. It largely depends on your perspective of the events leading up to the morning of June 28 and how you wish to interpret the Constitution of Honduras, and whether you give more weight to some Articles over others.

What I constantly find myself telling people who ask for my opinion about the political crisis in Honduras is, "Look, it's not black or white... mostly, there's a lot of grey." I have come to the conclusion that it is relatively useless to keep banging our heads together trying to convince each other of the exclusive righteousness of our views. It is enough to truly listen to one another without prejudging and without becoming enraged at each other. It is enough to cultivate the ability to simply agree to disagree, because then we allow ourselves some room to keep talking to each other.

It is precisely our efforts to try and convince each other that it was or was not a coup that seem to make it impossible for people to listen to one another. There are countless examples of friends, relatives, and colleagues in Honduras, and abroad, for whom calm discussions about Mr. Zelaya are impossible because they touch such a raw nerve that those involved suddenly become hostile, seemingly negating all the personal bonds that may have been built up over years. When Porfirio Lobo, who was elected as the new president of Honduras on November 29, 2009, acknowledged in a CNN interview in May 21, 2010 that Mr. Zelaya's overthrow was a coup, it cost him a great deal of political capital.   His willingness to shift from the standard party line that what occurred was a constitutional transition of power was treated as heresy by some.

It is unclear yet how many enemies President Lobo created for himself when he responded in the affirmative to reporter José Levi's question, "Was what occurred in Honduras a coup d'état?"   Given President Lobo's public revelation on June 8 that he had proof of a coup in the works against him, it is easy to speculate that at least a few people may not have been overjoyed with his position.

The disagreements over the terminology used to describe the removal of Mr. Zelaya would not be nearly so bad if the arguments that took place were reasonable and well crafted. Most of them are not.   They are often little more than shouting matches, with one side accusing the other of being *golpistas* or *fascistas* and the other side yelling back *"Chávistas"* or *"comunistas"*.

At a rally in front of the White House a few weeks after Mr. Zelaya's overthrow, I heard Hondurans chanting over and over again, "Democracy yes, communism no!"   It was as if the Cold War had not ended two decades ago.   It did not seem to matter that the words were nonsensical... they were meant to glorify anyone who was against Mr. Zelaya and demonize anyone who even vaguely supported him or sympathized with some of his policies.   It was meant to send the message, "Either you're with us (the good guys) or you're against us (the bad guys)", and reminded me of how often people choose to rely on labels rather than thoughtful discussion to make their points.   Once you label someone, then that person eternally becomes the enemy with whom you cannot talk or even sit down and have a cup of coffee.   This is what has happened in Honduras, making it extremely difficult to achieve true national reconciliation.

A vastly more interesting and possibly more productive conversation than the coup versus not-a-coup debate is the question of whether or not Mr. Zelaya deserved to be removed from power. From this perspective, there is the potential to elevate the conversation from a labeling game to a serious discussion about the pros and cons of the events that led to Mr. Zelaya's downfall, and thus hopefully to an understanding of how to avoid their recurrence in the future.

I have many reasons for believing the ousting of Mr. Zelaya was a "good coup", but my main reason is that the man committed the unpardonable sin of purposely pitting one segment of Honduran society against another. He blamed one class of people for all of Honduras' problems. By painting an evil image of the "elite" in the minds of the poor and middle classes, he sought to stir up anger and hate among the masses, within communities, and within families in service of some vague, poorly articulated notion he conjured up to incite a revolution in Honduras.

While I share the view that the status quo in Honduras is unsustainable and has to change, Mr. Zelaya's tactics for bringing about transformation of the country were irresponsible and dangerous because their ultimate goal was to divide, destroy, and re-invent the government from scratch. He talked often about "re-founding" Honduras, and saw himself as some sort of an historic founding father figure. Making it all even more surreal was the sense that Mr. Zelaya was improvising as he went along. Mr. Zelaya never presented a carefully planned long-term strategy or vision – no details of a blueprint for what Honduras should look like in the future. He offered only slogans and careless promises, mixed into a never-ending propaganda campaign, but expressed no interest in governing, and exhibited limited ability to do so. He portrayed himself as the heroic *caudillo* that would finally succeed in changing Honduras when so many who had come before had failed. The exorbitant price that he would extract from Honduran society did not seem to matter to Mr. Zelaya.

I closely tracked the events in Honduras leading up to June 28. I read all of the Spanish-language newspapers and exchanged hundreds of telephone calls, e-mails and postings on my Facebook page with countless people in Honduras and around the world about the evolving political crisis. While it may come as a surprise to many, the crisis did not begin when Mr. Zelaya was arrested and unceremoniously flown to Costa Rica. The crisis had been brewing for many months. Some of my exchanges led me to write essays, which were ultimately published as editorial pieces in *Honduras Weekly*. This book is a compilation of these essays, accompanied in some cases by personal notes conveying thoughts that either prompted me to write the essay or were follow-up thoughts inspired by the essay and written at a later date.

TIMELINE OF NOTABLE EVENTS

2008

August 25: Honduras becomes a member of the Bolivarian Alliance for the Americas (ALBA).

September 19: Hugo Llorens presents his credentials as the new Ambassador of the United States to Honduras to President Manuel Zelaya.

November 11: Zelaya announces a non-binding opinion poll to determine public support for a proposed referendum known as *la cuarta urna* (fourth ballot box) to vote on whether or not to review and rewrite the Constitution of Honduras. *La cuarta urna* referendum was to be held the same day as the national elections planned for November 29, 2009.

December 24: Zelaya issues Executive Decree 374-08 raising the minimum wage by 60 percent, effective January 1, 2009.

2009

March 23: Zelaya issues Executive Decree PCM–05–2009 calling for an opinion poll to determine public support for the establishment of a National Constituent Assembly to review and rewrite the Constitution. The order instructs the National Statistics Institute (INE) to hold the poll no later than June 28, 2009.

May 19:	The Public Ministry of Honduras declares the opinion poll illegal and petitions the Supreme Court of Justice of Honduras to suspend it.
May 20:	The Attorney General of Honduras declares the opinion poll illegal.
May 27:	The Supreme Court declares the opinion poll unconstitutional and orders its suspension and an injunction against anyone participating in it.
June 24:	Zelaya fires Honduras' head of the Armed Forces, General Romeo Vásquez, after he refused an order to disobey the Supreme Court's injunction and have Honduran soldiers distribute ballots for the opinion poll and provide security.
June 25:	The Supreme Court declares the firing of General Vásquez illegal and orders his immediate reinstatement. Zelaya leads a mob to Hernán Acosta Mejia Air Base and confiscates ballots impounded, by the Supreme Electoral Tribunal (TSE), meant for the opinion poll set for June 28. National Congress of Honduras appoints commission to investigate administrative conduct of Zelaya.
June 26:	The Public Ministry accuses Zelaya before the Supreme Court of abuse of power and treason. Supreme Court votes unanimously against Zelaya and orders his arrest. Supreme Court sends document (PCSJ-451-2009) to other Supreme Courts in Central America advising

them of its decision to declare the opinion poll unconstitutional.

June 27:
The Honduran government's official newspaper, *La Gaceta*, publishes the text of the questions that will appear in the opinion poll the next day. The questions ask voters whether or not they would support holding *la cuarta urna* referendum on November 29 and, if so, whether or not they would support the establishment of a National Constituent Assembly to review and rewrite the Constitution.

June 28:
Zelaya is arrested by Honduran soldiers on orders from the Supreme Court and flown to San José, Costa Rica.

June 30:
The General Assembly of the United Nations (UN) unanimously votes to condemn the overthrow of Zelaya and calls for his immediate and unconditional reinstatement.

July 3:
The Secretary General of the Organization of American States (OAS), José Miguel Insulza, visits Tegucigalpa to insist on Zelaya's reinstatement. The government of interim president Roberto Micheletti refuses.

July 5:
Zelaya flies to Tegucigalpa aboard a private business jet on loan from President Hugo Chávez of Venezuela and attempts to land at Toncontín International Airport. Honduran soldiers block the runway preventing the aircraft from landing. A confrontation develops between soldiers guarding the airport and thousands of Zelaya supporters. Isis

Obed Murillo, 19, is shot by a soldier and becomes the first person to die in the escalating political crisis. The OAS votes to suspend Honduras from the organization.

July 7:   Zelaya meets with US Secretary of State Hillary Clinton in Washington, DC. Clinton announces Costa Rican President Óscar Arias will oversee mediation talks in San José, Costa Rica between representatives of Zelaya and Micheletti.

July 9:   Delegations representing Zelaya and Micheletti meet in San José to begin negotiations on ending the political crisis.

July 22:   Arias makes a final proposal to the Zelaya and Micheletti delegations participating in the San José mediation talks, and says the OAS will have to settle the dispute if there is no agreement.

July 23:   Arias mediation talks end in failure.

July 24   Zelaya takes brief symbolic and highly publicized step into Honduran territory near the Nicaraguan border town of Ocotal.

September 3:   The US terminates aid to Honduras.

September 21: Zelaya secretly returns to Tegucigalpa and takes refuge in the Brazilian embassy in Tegucigalpa.

October 7: The Micheletti government initiates a new round of talks – the *Diálogo Guaymuras* – with Zelaya representatives in Tegucigalpa.

October 28:	A high-level US delegation arrives in Tegucigalpa to help jumpstart the stalled *Diálogo Guaymuras* talks between represent-tatives of Zelaya and the Micheletti govern-ment. The delegation includes US Assistant Secretary of State for Western Hemisphere Affairs Thomas Shannon, Deputy Assistant Secretary of State for Western Hemisphere Affairs Craig Kelly, and White House Special Assistant for Western Hemisphere Affairs Dan Restrepo.
October 30:	The Tegucigalpa-San José Accord is signed by representatives of Zelaya and interim presi-dent Roberto Micheletti setting forth pro-visions to end the political crisis in Honduras.
November 3:	US Assistant Secretary of State for Western Hemisphere Affairs, Thomas Shannon, states in an interview with CNN that the US govern-ment will respect the outcome of Congress's vote on the reinstatement of Zelaya.
November 29:	Porfirio Lobo elected president of Honduras, winning 56 percent of the popular vote.
December 2:	Congress votes 111–14 against reinstating Zelaya.

2010

January 26:	Congress passes an amnesty decree for all political offenses committed against Honduras between January 1, 2009 and January 27, 2010, including efforts to alter the country's form of government through the

installation of *la cuarta urna*. The decree covers acts of sedition and terrorism, inciting public insurrection, vandalism, conspiring to distribute arms, and abuse of power. It does not include criminal acts such as misappropriation of public funds, theft, and corruption.

January 27: President-elect Porfirio Lobo inaugurated as president of Honduras. Lobo allows Zelaya to leave the Brazilian embassy and fly to the Dominican Republic under the status of "Distinguished Guest", commencing a self-imposed exile. Honduran Congress votes to withdraw Honduras from ALBA.

January 29: The US announces it will resume economic assistance to Honduras.

February 2: The US restarts security assistance to Honduras.

March 5: Zelaya meets with President Hugo Chávez in Caracas and is appointed chief political consultant for Petrocaribe. President Lobo meets with Secretary of State Clinton in Guatemala City to discuss US-Honduras bilateral relations.

March 11: Zelaya's chief aide, Rasel Tomé returns to Honduras from the Dominican Republic.

March 24: The OAS re-elects José Miguel Insulza as Secretary General.

April 19: Zelaya's wife, Xiomara, returns to Honduras from the Dominican Republic.

April 26:	President Obama speaks to President Lobo by telephone and promises support to deal with crime and immigration issues.
May 4:	The Honduras Truth and National Reconciliation Commission is formally inaugurated by the Lobo government. The Commission is tasked to submit a final report by January 2011.
May 5:	President Lobo confirms the appointment of Jorge Ramón Hernández Alcerro as Honduras' new ambassador to the US.
May 13:	Zelaya meets with President Daniel Ortega of Nicaragua in Managua and announces a plan for national reconciliation that barters support for Honduras' readmission into the OAS in exchange for amnesty for alleged crimes during his administration and recognition of the National Resistance Front Against the Coup d'État (*la Resistencia*) as a political party.
May 21:	President Porfirio Lobo acknowledges in an interview with CNN's José Levi that the overthrow of President Zelaya was a coup d'état. Lobo said, "Of course it was a coup. Call it whatever you want, but it was a coup."
June 7:	Secretary of State Clinton advocates for readmission of Honduras to the OAS at OAS General Assembly meeting in Lima, Perú.
June 8:	Zelaya urges former officials of his administration not to cooperate with the Truth and National Reconciliation Commission.

INTRODUCTION

On the evening of March 23, 2009, President Manuel Zelaya issued Executive Decree PCM–05–2009 declaring that citizens of Honduras should be allowed to vote on whether or not to establish a National Constituent Assembly (*la Constituyente*) to review and rewrite the country's Constitution. The Order specified the installation of a fourth ballot box (*la cuarta urna*) during the national elections, scheduled for November 29, 2009, so that citizens could vote on the Assembly proposal. President Zelaya announced that a non-binding *encuesta* (opinion poll), overseen by the National Statistics Institute (INE), should be held by June 28, 2009. Quoted in a Reuters news release, President Zelaya stated, "Society has gone through substantial changes in recent years that demand a new constitutional framework more in tandem with the current national situation."

The Order and the decision by President Zelaya to hold a preliminary opinion poll quickly sparked a wave of criticism throughout Honduras. The move was decried as part of a strategy to allow him to remain in office past his term, set to end on January 27, 2010, by rewriting the Constitution to his benefit... much in the same way that Presidents Hugo Chávez and Evo Morales had done in Venezuela and Bolivia. The Constitution provides for a single presidential term of four years. That's it. The attempt by President Zelaya to change this key provision of the Constitution created fear that he was seeking to change the rules of the game in midstream in order to remain in power indefinitely – a phenomenon known in Latin America as *Continuismo*.

Members of both the conservative Nationalist party and President Zelaya's own Liberal Party came out in strong opposition to both the fourth ballot box and the opinion poll. President Zelaya's own Attorney General and the Public Ministry declared them to be illegal. Honduras' Supreme Court declared them unconstitutional. In a functional government with a responsible president, that should have been the end of it. Rather than respecting the rulings of the established democratic institutions, however, President Zelaya pushed ahead with apparent disregard for any potential negative consequences.

Honduras' Constitution was written in 1982 when the country was emerging from years of military rule. Since then, Honduras has experienced peaceful and predictable transitions of presidential power every four years. Fiddling with the Constitution carried the potential of ushering in a new era of political instability that the country could ill afford, given the unceasing and sizeable social and economic problems that plague Honduran society. There was understandable apprehension that rewriting the Constitution could immediately and unalterably strengthen the hand of the president and political party in power, thereby placing Honduras' democratic system in jeopardy.

But there was also concern that Honduras' nagging problems were, at least partly, structural in nature and thus that the system of government had to be revamped in order to allow for solutions to be effectively implemented. There was a general feeling that Honduras needed a particularly strong executive with a wide range of powers allowing for infinitely greater flexibility to deal with Honduras' often dysfunctional public institutions, laws, and customs. That was the dilemma. How could you go about changing the social and economic status quo in Honduras – widely perceived as unjust and inherently destabilizing – with political institutions (particularly the presidency) that were painfully weak and ineffective?

CLOUDY SKIES

June 26, 2009

The weather forecast for Tegucigalpa
through Tuesday calls for thundershowers.

Maybe that's a good thing...
help keep people off the streets.

Leading a Polarized Society

June 2, 2009

A country can do very little if it is polarized. If there is division within a society, then it is nearly impossible to arrive at a consensus on decisions about problems and issues that need to be addressed. There is stagnation – an inability to act constructively. What prevail are criticism, accusation, bickering, and protest. If there is division, then mostly what is present is misunderstanding, distrust, and fear. Anger and disorder reign, and this leads to a loss of clear thinking and inspiration. Without this clarity of thought and vision, there can be no integrated, comprehensive strategy for how to lead. Thus, leadership must begin by creating unity and harmony. To seek another way is something else. But it is not leadership.

Honduras is the fourth poorest country in the Western Hemisphere. Only the people of Haiti, Nicaragua, and Guyana find themselves worse off. More than three-quarters of Honduras' population is poor and struggling to survive, much less get ahead. The country is already seriously divided along social classes. The wealthy make up a tiny portion of the society. There is a very small, unstable and relatively uninfluential middle class. The country has always had political divisions, but during the past three decades, the political party establishments have played by a set of rules that have allowed for timely and peaceful transitions of power. The military has

1

become more professional and has been happy to stay out of politics. Now, something is happening in Honduras that is threatening the relative political calm that has existed for the past three decades.

The country is becoming severely fractured politically and there is a growing sense of mistrust and disorder because the traditional rules of the political game are in the process of being changed. Whatever illusion of unity and harmony Honduras has had is quickly fading. The country must try to regain that illusion because it does not have the luxury of being distracted from its sizeable and growing array of social problems. The idea that changing a document such as the Constitution of a country (to allow for who knows what) is the "silver bullet" that will make everything better begs the question, "Are most of the faults for Honduras' problems in our Constitution or within ourselves?"

NOTES

1. It is important to speak the truth always, but truth isn't always absolute and static. It is often relative and fluid. Thus, it is wise to be empathetic and try to appreciate the truth of others. That is the way to engage in a conversation that may lead to positive and constructive action. At the moment, everyone is blaming each other. Everyone is talking past each other. These are all distractions that lead nowhere. And the poor remain poor.

2. During his presidential campaign, Barack Obama emphasized that "words matter" because they affect the way people think and act. The divisions in Honduras originate from both the inequalities that exist and the tone of public and private discourse. If the words and tone are filled with anger, fear and distrust, then no policy, no strategy, regardless of how wonderful, will succeed because there will be no unity. Being right or wrong counts for nothing if a society, a community, or a family are in conflict.

3. Dissent is one of the hallmarks of democratic societies. Most people in Honduras tend to agree on the central problems and the importance of effectively addressing them, but they disagree on strategy. What is crucial right now is first to unite the country and deal with the anger and distrust that seems to be growing. Otherwise, there will never be the means to deal with the problems that the Honduran people face every day, and we'll be talking about the same stuff 20 years from now.

A Permanent State of Protest

June 5, 2009

A large portion of Honduras' population spends a huge portion of its time protesting and striking. People protest that they haven't been paid for months. They protest against the rise in food and fuel prices. They protest against violence and crime. They protest against government inaction and corruption. They protest against foreign mining companies that are poisoning the rivers. Taxi drivers strike. Teachers strike. Bus drivers strike. Nurses strike. Doctors strike. Indigenous tribes strike. Truck drivers strike. Students strike. Apart from soccer, protesting and striking are the national pastimes of Honduras.

When people protest and strike, it is because they want to be heard. The normal channels of communication have failed, leading to a sense that there is no alternative other than to amass in public. By that time, so much of the trust and goodwill between people have already eroded. Building this trust and goodwill, and developing a sense of wanting to work together for a common cause, is the basis for moving to resolve the problems and issues of the country. This cannot be done by pitting one segment of the society against another, claiming sole mastery of the truth, and pointing accusatory fingers, but rather by finding creative ways to gradually heal the divisions.

Protests and strikes are part of the democratic process and certainly a right within free societies. The problem is when protests and strikes are constant and the issues never get addressed to everyone's full satisfaction. Thus, in the end they tend to seriously disrupt the society and hurt people who are not part of the squabble, particularly students who simply want to receive an education, patients who require medical care, and people who use public transportation to get to work.

NOTES

1. Imagine if you had a dollar for every minute that every Honduran spent marching in protest against or in favor of something during the past week. Imagine a dollar for every minute that every Honduran spent marching in the past 20 years. Imagine a dollar for every minute that every child in Honduras has spent at home or on the streets when they should have been in the classroom learning. Honduras would be a financially rich country... if you imagined all those dollars.

2. The main problem in Honduras is not corruption or even poverty. The main problem is poor governance, which in turn leads to corruption and poverty. The people of Honduras must find a way to elect capable leaders with good visions and workable strategies to implement those visions without dividing their society and alienating people and institutions that are needed to get things done. Otherwise, there is chaos and an endless exchange of simplistic and partisan arguments about why one side is completely right and the other side is completely wrong.

3. The majority of the people in Honduras feel they have no voice. This creates a sense of powerlessness, which sometimes manifests itself in street protests and highway blockages and vandalism. Somehow, Honduras has to establish a legitimate and honest process that allows people to... yes, "vent"... and be heard. This will hopefully create awareness. And the awareness will hopefully create compassion, which may lead to the implementation of helpful responses to problems.

EL PUEBLO

June 6, 2009

The following quote from President Manuel Zelaya was published in today's *La Tribuna* newspaper:

"El no quiere que se haga la encuesta, le tiene miedo al pueblo, el que se somete a vivir en un sistema democrático tiene que respetar al pueblo y ese es un principio superior a cualquier político, superior al presidente, superior al Congreso Nacional, la democracia directa es un nuevo escenario de democracia que vamos a establecer en Honduras, el pueblo lo quiere, yo se lo voy a permitir, yo lo voy a apoyar al pueblo para que ejerza ese derecho y que nunca más en la historia de este país se vuelvan a hacer cosas sin consultas del pueblo."

The translation goes... "Whoever does not want the opinion poll to be held is afraid of the people. Whoever wishes to live in a democratic system has to respect the people, and that is a principle that stands above any politician, above the president, above Congress. Direct democracy is a new democratic landscape that we will establish in Honduras. The people want it and I am going to permit it. I am going to support the people so that that right can be exercised so that never again in the history of this country will things be done without consulting the people."

This statement is extremely interesting, and goes to the heart of what the president seems to want to do in Honduras. It is precisely this that is causing such a stir at the moment. Some of the key phrases in this quote are:

> *"respetar al pueblo"* (respect the people) ... *"un principio superior a qualquier politico, superior al presidente, superior al Congreso Nacional"* (a principle above any politician, above the president, above Congress) ... *"democracia directa"* (direct democracy) ... *"un nuevo escenario de democracia"* (a new democratic landscape)

It sounds good, but no one really knows what it all means or who would be in charge of managing this new system. While the intentions might be noble, given the continuing plight of the vast portion of Honduran society, the potential for even more chaos in Honduras would be worse than mass poverty, because you cannot deal effectively with mass poverty in a state of chaos.

"El Pueblo" or "The People" is a wonderful concept, but it can also be a very divisive concept if it is used to pit the masses who are poor against the relatively few who represent the middle and upper classes. All the classes of Honduras represent Honduras, and they need to live together, work together, and find common ground.

Additionally, "The People" cannot rule the country directly. That is why democracies establish representative governments with different branches charged with doing very specialized things. Honduras has a broken democracy that does not adequately represent the needs and desires of most Hondurans. But the way to fix something is to repair it, not throw it away and assume that the new product will work better.

A broken democracy leaves much to be desired, but there are many worse social systems. So fix it, don't scrap it. Fixing something may seem a lot harder and demand more creative energy than buying into something totally new. There are no guarantees that the tinkering and fine-tuning will fix the problems. Neither are there guarantees when starting from scratch.

MEL'S BIG FAVOR

June 23, 2009

Albeit in a clumsy and reckless sort of way, President Zelaya is doing Honduran society a big favor. Whether by intent or side effect, he is reminding the powers-that-be in Honduras that the status quo must change. The question now is, "Who will be the promoter and arbiter of this change?" Will it be an individual with an overly generous concentration of power and tenure or will it be all three branches of the government in equal partnership with the business community and civil society? Will it be by force or by consensus?

What model of "participatory democracy" will Honduras adopt? One where an executive proposes and rules by public referendum or one where all segments of society participate selflessly for the good of the whole? There are problems with both models. In the former, you have to trust that power will not be abused and that referendums will not be staged or manipulated. In the latter, you have to convince people to go against their natural tendency to mostly look out for their own narrow and immediate interests... an extremely tough sell.

While Honduras seems more polarized than at any time in recent memory, the reality is that you cannot really have a country that is united and living in peace when three-quarters of its population is poor and has no voice (at least not one that is heard) and little hope. Mr. Zelaya is merely raising the stakes.

NOTES

If hundreds of thousands of Hondurans can mobilize to protest and demonstrate (both in favor of and against something or someone) on the streets of Honduras' cities and in the countryside, then it begins to disprove the theory that Hondurans suffer from apathy. The question is now, "Can we mobilize the same energy and enthusiasm to work together in positive ways to change Honduras by volunteering daily to help those in need?"

A LITTLE PROBLEM OF TRUST

June 24, 2009

While all the commotion in Honduras these days is focused on *la cuarta urna*, the reality is that the main problem is one of trust. While nearly everyone in Honduras believes that the status quo in the country is unacceptable, there is disagreement on how and what to change. In other words, "What should the process for change be and what should Honduras look like in the future?" Theoretically, these are the type of questions that *la cuarta urna* would help answer.

The problem is that because of his style of leadership, his personal associations, the content and tone of his rhetoric, and a certain lack of clarity of his intentions (How exactly does a "participatory democracy" actually work?), President Zelaya has failed to inspire confidence and trust among large segments of Honduras' middle and upper classes. The daily gatherings of thousands and tens of thousands of people expressing their opposition to *la cuarta urna* and *continuismo* and support for democracy, freedom, and peace are a visual testament to his relative lack of success.

Clearly, there are other segments of the population that do trust Mr. Zelaya and believe his intentions are genuine, selfless, and primarily focused on changing the power balance in Honduras so that the poor and powerless can have better access to the resources of the country. If you are frustrated that nothing ever seems to change for the better in Honduras, regardless of which party is in office, then it's understandable to want to opt for anything that might break the stalemate... even if it's risky. After all, what do you really have to lose if you already lack hope?

At this stage, it is probably too late for Mr. Zelaya to gain the confidence and trust of those who do not already feel this for him. Those who oppose him are mobilized and fired up, and it is now more of a personal matter against Mr. Zelaya. The belief that simply staying in power is what is at the heart of Mr. Zelaya's intentions has become widespread to the point that the message about the unacceptability of the status quo in Honduras is being drowned out. It is too bad that in political campaigns the message often tends to cede ground to animosity toward an individual.

Mr. Zelaya still has time to get back on message. He has the enviable advantage of having gotten the public's attention. But he should accept (and convey to the public his acceptance) that he cannot change the rules of the game in midstream and try to remain in power. The memory of past dictatorships is still too recent for many Hondurans.

It may be that the Articles of the Constitution that deal with term limits and the way in which Honduras is governed will eventually need to be revised. But it doesn't seem possible for this to happen under Mr. Zelaya's administration without a continued deterioration of the situation in Honduras... to the point where the country becomes completely ungovernable.

NOTES

1. It is irresponsible to force a referendum when there is such a clear threat of public disorder and violence on both sides. All it takes is for one person to be killed on the streets, and suddenly you have escalated a political squabble between the president and the other institutions of government into a full-blown crisis.

2. Do referendums open the way for dictatorships? If so, would a country like Honduras fare better under a benevolent quasi-socialist dictator whose main interest (at least initially) is to care for the needs of the poor and powerless? Or is Honduras better off with its current broken version of representative democracy, where freedom and civil liberties are relatively meaningless concepts to more than three-quarters of its people who spend most of their waking hours just trying to find enough food to feed their families?

3. An administration can do very little in four short years. In order for a president and his or her cabinet to make a real impact in Honduras, they probably do need to have the option of running for a second term. At least one basis for the one-term limitation is that there is very little confidence in the abilities and ethics of political leaders in Honduras, and so the guiding principle seems to be to elect the individual who will do the least amount of harm and steal the least amount of money from the country, rather than elect the person with the best vision and with the greatest ability to implement it.

A Participatory Democracy

June 24, 2009

There's a certain attraction to a "participatory democracy" versus a "representative democracy". In theory, a participatory democracy (or "direct democracy") sounds good because it allows more direct participation by its citizens in the decision-making process of a country rather than leaving the actual governing to politicians who supposedly represent their interests. It is an attempt to transfer the balance of power more toward the people themselves than to a select number of representatives, as exists in a representative democracy.

One of the underlying assumptions of a participatory democracy is that the only way to effectively combat corruption and an over-concentration of political power within a society is to disperse it. But this idea assumes that only people at the top of the political chain are corruptible. The concept seems to neglect the reality that wherever there is an opportunity to gain political power, there will also be opportunities for corruption.

Simply dispersing political power will, in and of itself, not solve the problems of corruption, inaction, and incompetence. Instead, this transfer of power may actually produce more chaos because power would be handed over to people who are unprepared to make well-informed decisions.

A participatory democracy might work in a society that is highly educated and motivated and has wide and free access to information and communications technologies (ICT) that allow for quick collection of data, effective mobilization and organization, and an efficient infrastructure for relaying decisions. None of this exists in Honduras, making it entirely likely that those charged with "managing" the envisioned participatory democracy would find the system too cumbersome and thus too tempting to try and manipulate.

Other than Sweden, there is no model for a successful participatory democracy on a national scale. The jury is still out on the Venezuelan model. Venezuela under Hugo Chávez is no utopia, and it has the huge advantage of possessing the world's seventh largest oil reserves – enough to last 88 years.

Whether Honduras becomes a participatory democracy or remains a representative democracy, ultimately it will not make much difference to the average poor person so long as the country's education system continues to be neglected. It is only a radically improved, super-charged education system that will change Honduras for the better. This is the best and more direct way to empower people, ensure that resources (including political capital) are more evenly distributed, and guarantee that they will participate in the democratic process... whichever version is chosen.

NOTES

1. You cannot impose a sophisticated system like participatory democracy that requires a self-sufficient population on a country like Honduras, which has an extremely poor education system and horrendous cultural diseases like *machismo* that stunt its growth. Honduras has a long way to go to adequately teach its children and adults how to read, think critically, practice good decision-making, hold productive meetings, and use communications and information technologies.

2. There seems to be no light at the end of the tunnel to this problem of education in Honduras. If teachers in Honduras are more beholden to their unions than to their students, then the students will lose out every time, and the future of the country will become dimmer and dimmer. The development of Honduras is being held hostage to the interests of the teachers unions. This has to change because, in the end, no one benefits from an uneducated population.

EXPERIMENTATION

June 25, 2009

Change cannot be forced upon Honduras without utterly destroying the fabric of Honduran society by pitting party against party, class against class, family against family, and sector against sector. Democracies cannot be governed successfully over the long-term from either the far left or the far right. Eventually, the pendulum will swing the other way and whatever perceived or real progress was made before will be washed away by a new movement that will seek to make up for lost time and bruised egos. As in a game of chess, you stand the best chance of consistently winning when you control the center of the board. You have a better view from the middle and you have access to more paths and more players.

The United States is emerging from eight years of right-wing rule. It is a divided nation that is still involved in two wars, carries a massive foreign debt of more than $10 trillion and annual deficits approaching $1 trillion, has a myriad of long-neglected domestic issues which include a collapsing transportation infrastructure; a population that suffers from obesity, drug abuse, and stress; an inefficient and wasteful healthcare delivery system; out-of-control special interests that corrupt government; an unregulated and greedy financial community; high rates of personal and corporate bankruptcies... and on and on.

Despite all of this, the US has a huge reservoir of resources that it can put into play to begin to address its problems. It has a well-educated population. It has world-class competitive corporations, universities, and research institutes. It has tens of thousands of non-profit foundations and well-funded churches and well-endowed philanthropic organizations. It has tremendous entrepreneurial spirit and creative talent. It has cutting edge technologies. It has a professional civil service and a relatively unpoliticized and responsive judicial system. It still has a fairly large, influential, and powerful middle class.

Honduras has no such reservoir. It does not have the luxury of throwing caution to the wind and undertaking experiments that divide and polarize the nation by governing without consensus from one end of the spectrum or the other. All of Honduras' limited human capital has to be tapped if the country ever hopes to emerge intact from endemic poverty and injustice.

Don't Blame the Military

June 29, 2009

In several interviews following his arrest and expulsion from Honduras, President Zelaya has portrayed himself as an innocent victim of a coup d'état. His view has been amplified by foreign leaders such as Presidents Hugo Chávez of Venezuela, Daniel Ortega of Nicaragua, and Rafael Correa of Ecuador.

The impression that this view has conveyed to the world is that the arrest by Honduran troops during the morning of June 28 signaled a dangerous return to the 1960s and 1970s when rogue generals such as Oswaldo López Arellano and Juan Alberto Melgar Castro regularly overthrew presidents by force and ruled Honduras through military *juntas*. This impression is inaccurate. Honduras' Armed Forces have invested much time, effort and financial capital during the past three decades to reform themselves and emerge as a professional and apolitical institution.

The decision to arrest Mr. Zelaya was made by Honduras' Supreme Court and backed by a Congress that is nearly unanimous in its opposition to Mr. Zelaya. The military, led by the head of the Joint Chiefs, General Romeo Vásquez Velásquez, moved against the President only after the Supreme Court, the Congress, the Public Ministry, the Attorney General, and the Commissioner for Human Rights determined that a series of political maneuvers by Mr. Zelaya were illegal and had the potential to cause severe public unrest and lead to Mr. Zelaya trying to remain in office past his current four-year term. The Constitution of Honduras prohibits second terms for presidents.

General Vásquez was placed in the unenviable position of having to choose whether to be loyal to his Commander in Chief or to the Constitution, as interpreted by the Judiciary and Legislative branches of the government. Mr. Zelaya weakened his own credibility with the military by publicly sacking General Vásquez for refusing to support a legally questionable referendum that had been scheduled to begin the morning of his arrest. The dismissal of General Vásquez led the heads of Honduras' three services of the Armed Forces, as well as the civilian Minister of Defense, to resign in a show of solidarity.

The reality is that the Honduran military found itself in a no-win situation by a continually escalating conflict involving Honduras' three branches of government. The inability of Honduras' civilian political leaders to establish a civil dialogue on how to resolve their differences forced General Vásquez and his staff to choose their allegiance. Ultimately, the general opted for what he viewed as defending the Constitution. If there are any "victims" in this chapter of Honduran history, it is the Armed Forces, not the politicians.

NOTES

1. Tens of thousands of Hondurans have marched in the streets to express their support for peace and democracy, and oppose Mr. Zelaya's moves to change the Constitution. Congress, the Supreme Court, the Attorney General, the Human Rights Commissioner, the Catholic Church, evangelical churches, and the business community have all joined in. The voices of these people count as much or more than all the ambassadors at the United Nations who pretend to know what is right for Honduras.

2. Just because 192 governments of the world agree to condemn the arrest and exile of President Zelaya doesn't mean they are right. By that same reasoning, the 120 of the 128 *diputados* in the Honduran Congress who voted to appoint Mr. Micheletti as Mr. Zelaya's replacement would also be right. It has nothing to do with numbers. It is possible for a minority of one to be right. Furthermore, there is a huge amount of hypocrisy within the UN, given that most of the member states are not democracies. Their main reason for the condemnation has nothing to do with democracy, and everything to do with discouraging the overthrow of standing governments, regardless of whether they are democratic, socialist, or dictatorships. Cuba is an oppressive dictatorship, so its condemnation of the coup has no value.

3. What in the world was José Miguel Insulza thinking? He gave the interim government of Honduras a 72-hour ultimatum to reverse its stance with regard to Mr. Zelaya, and then showed up in Tegucigalpa stating that he will not negotiate. Now he has returned empty-handed and looks extremely weak. The only thing he accomplished was to make the interim government ever more defiant. The next step will be for the OAS to suspend Honduras from that body, which will matter little to most Hondurans. Mr. Insulza's complete and utter miscalculation (not to mention arrogance) of the level of unity within the interim government and the mood of a large portion of the Honduran population does nothing to enhance the reputation of the OAS.

4. How ironic is it that the OAS is entertaining suspending Honduras for what has happened when this organization only a few weeks ago voted to readmit Cuba. Perhaps there is a

statute of limitations for countries that overthrow governments by force and violence? So maybe Cuba is now considered a "democracy"?

5. General Vásquez said they decided to carry Mr. Zelaya out of the country because they were concerned about public order. One of the main reasons the Supreme Court (with the support of the Congress) ordered the Armed Forces to arrest President Zelaya was directly related to his use of the mob on Thursday, June 25 to break into Hernán Acosta Mejia Air Base to retrieve the boxes of ballots for the opinion poll on June 28. The Supreme Electoral Tribunal had impounded those boxes. Mr. Zelaya went against that impoundment order and intimidated General Prince (the commander of the base) to open the gates and let him and hundreds of his followers onto the base. It was at that point the military and other government institutions began to fear how far Mr. Zelaya would go in using the mob as his shield. Had the military tried to arrest Mel and keep him in a prison in Honduras, there was clearly the potential for violent riots greater than what the country had experienced so far.

6. It has become evident that the Supreme Court only ordered Mr. Zelaya's arrest, not his expulsion, and that taking him out of the country may have been illegal. It would appear that Mr. Zelaya has a reasonable case to make in his defense.

ÓSCAR ARIAS IS NOT THE SAVIOR

July 8, 2009

Both the interim government and Mr. Zelaya have embraced the offer by President Óscar Arias of Costa Rica to mediate and help contain the political crisis in Honduras. It is not surprising that the US government has blessed this path. But the people of Honduras should not be seduced into viewing Mr. Arias as the man who will find a way to solve the true conflict that exists in Honduras.

Óscar Rafael de Jesús Arias Sánchez is a brilliant man and an excellent leader. He received the 1987 Nobel Peace Prize for his work in promoting democracy and negotiating peace in Central America during the 1980s, which was a decade of turmoil throughout the region. The negotiations led to the signing of what is known as the Esquipulas II Accords.

While President Arias may well succeed in helping the opposing sides in Honduras reach a deal that will prevent an outbreak of serious violence and instability in the country in the near-term, this gentleman cannot resolve the underlying social problems that created the environment for the current crisis. A situation where three-quarters of Hondurans are poor and vast wealth is concentrated in the hands of less than ten percent of the population is unsustainable. This is the real crisis in Honduras. Mr. Zelaya was simply a wake-up call.

If Honduran society responds after the immediate threat is over by going back to business as usual, then nothing will have been accomplished. The next time a threat to the relative peace and democracy emerges in Honduras, the country may not be so fortunate.

One of the lessons to bear in mind is that, for the majority of Hondurans, peace and democracy have never really existed. Those are concepts that only make sense to people who don't have to worry about where their next meal will come from or how they will find help for their sick child. Mr. Zelaya represented hope for many of these dispossessed people. It may have been a false hope, but nonetheless, it was hope.

Regardless of his vague self-comparisons with Jesus Christ, Mr. Zelaya is obviously not the savior of Honduras, and neither is Mr. Arias. Only the Honduran people can save their society by, as Gandhi said, "being the change you want to see in the world".

NOTES

There are many to blame for this sad episode in Honduras' history, not the least of which are all those who have long ignored the plight of the vast portion of Honduras' population. But contrary to the accusations of Mr. Zelaya, who himself is part of the "elite" class he enjoys castigating for effect, the blame is shared by every Honduran who does not lend a hand to his or her neighbor, including all of "El Pueblo" – the poor, the middle class, and the wealthy. It is shared by everyone who refuses to be humble and believes their way is the only way.

✠

TALKING TOUGH FROM A
POSITION OF WEAKNESS

July 16, 2009

As part of its negotiating package in Costa Rica, the interim government of Honduras has offered the possibility of moving its presidential elections from November 29 to an earlier date. It has also offered the possibility of amnesty to Mr. Zelaya for the numerous criminal charges that he is facing, including abuse of power and treason... not to mention the growing list of corruption-related activities of his administration that are being uncovered almost daily. Now, interim president Roberto Micheletti has offered to resign if it helps placate Mr. Zelaya and his supporters. The one point on which the interim government will not budge is the reinstatement of Mr. Zelaya as president of Honduras.

Mr. Zelaya's position has been a little less imaginative. The day before the talks in San José began, Mr. Zelaya said that he expected the process to be completed within 24 hours. He said that these were not negotiations, but rather a dialogue about making "arrangements" for his return to office. Throughout the first week of the talks, Mr. Zelaya continued to travel between Central America and the US aboard a business jet graciously provided by Mr. Chávez... holding press conferences and reading ominous-sounding warnings. He threatened to punish the *golpistas* upon his return to Honduras, and issued an ultimatum threatening that if the talks in Costa Rica did not produce a plan for his reinstatement within a few days then he would resort to "other measures".

If you did not know any better, you would think that Mr. Zelaya is the one who is bargaining from a position of strength, and that it is the other side that finds itself in a desperate state. The reality is that Mr. Zelaya is the one without a party and without a country, living out of a suitcase. He is the one who is facing up to 20 years in prison. He is the one who is quickly fading from the headlines in the international press. He is the one who is starting to lose credibility as anything remotely resembling a serious person, given stunts like his flight aboard an unwelcome Venezuelan aircraft over Tegucigalpa that led to the death of 19-year old Isis Obed Murillo. Even comedian Jon Stewart has had a go at Mel.

Mr. Zelaya's latest contribution that will no doubt win accolades around the globe for its noblesse and creativity is to call for an "insurrection" in Honduras to pressure the interim government to give in. Insurrection? Sounds like something worth condemning, not cheering.

NOTES

1. The main concern with Mr. Zelaya's provocative flight to Tegucigalpa accompanied by the presidents of Argentina, Ecuador and Paraguay is that there was never an announcement about the trip's intent. If it is simply to demand that Mr. Zelaya be reinstated, then we are in for an unpleasant confrontation and stalemate at Toncontín airport... assuming of course that Honduran authorities give the chartered aircraft permission to land or even enter Honduran airspace.

2. This trip could potentially cause a regional military crisis, involving numerous nations of Latin America, including Argentina, Ecuador, Paraguay, and all of the ALBA nations. History is riddled with examples of a relatively minor and containable political crisis in a small nation quickly escalating into a broader military crisis drawing in more powerful countries. When President Correa of Ecuador says things like, "Honduras would be a good place to die", then it's time to worry. Whose agenda is on the table? Is it about preserving democracy in Honduras or is the country being used for broader regional political schemes? Is Mr. Zelaya being manipulated by powers that he does not understand?

3. It would be foolish for one or more of the ALBA countries to attempt to intervene militarily in Honduras, since they would only succeed in uniting the Honduran people. Suddenly, all the divisions created by Mr. Zelaya would disappear. The issue of the hybrid coup in Honduras would then take a back seat to the issue of interventionism.

4. Mr. Zelaya's live streaming commentary from his Venezuelan aircraft as he was flying above Tegucigalpa yesterday sounded very strange, to the point where people asked if he was "under the influence of something". Rather than sounding conciliatory and humble about the mistakes he has made, Mr. Zelaya sounded precisely like... well, a king demanding his throne back. At the same time, he is also denigrating those (the military) he wishes would switch their allegiance back to him by calling them "assassins". He has burned his bridges in Honduras, and so the idea of the interim government simply opting to bow to Mr. Zelaya seems remote. Mr. Zelaya is history.

✠

THE IRONY OF STRIKING FOR MEL

July 16, 2009

Egged on by Mel's recent call for an insurrection in Honduras, supporters of Mr. Zelaya have called for general labor strikes and the blocking of major roads. The idea of striking in favor of Mel is extremely ironic, given that Mr. Zelaya was himself the target of dozens of strikes throughout his three-and-a-half years as president. In fact, it is difficult to recall a president of Honduras who has had to confront as many strikes and demonstrations as Mr. Zelaya.

Part of the problem is that Mel has the unfortunate habit of promising the world, but when it comes time to deliver... nothing. This, of course, has the effect of aggravating people even more. Still, Mel continues to throw out promises like candy. People hold on to this false hope because it is better than no hope at all. The relationship is like that of an abusive husband who apologizes to his wife and promises never to beat her again. The wife believes him and takes him back, only to be abused again. The cycle repeats itself over and over with the hope by the wife that her husband truly loves her and will eventually change. But the abuse continues.

In August of 2006, some 61,000 teachers struck for two weeks, keeping 2.5 million children out of school. Approximately 20,000 teachers from all of Honduras' 18 departments arrived in Tegucigalpa and protested in front of the presidential offices, the Congress, and the Ministries of

Education and Finance. Twice they tried to occupy Toncontín airport. Instead of negotiating in good faith with the teachers, President Zelaya escalated the situation. The teachers were being housed at the University of Honduras, sleeping on old mattresses, and President Zelaya tried to intimidate and discourage them by having the water turned off at the university. This was in the middle of August.

To make matters worse, President Zelaya decided to take a trip to Nicaragua to ride his horse in a parade. What kind of president plays cowboy in a parade in Managua when he has thousands of disgruntled teachers waging havoc in Tegucigalpa?

This was one of the more obvious examples of Mr. Zelaya's exceptionally poor, deceptive and disingenuous leadership. Eventually, President Zelaya was forced to negotiate with some degree of seriousness, and an agreement was reached. In the years that followed, the teachers struck several more times against Mel because he failed to follow through with the promises he made.

NOTES

It is unfortunate that Manuel Zelaya has now become a kind of cult figure to hundreds and perhaps thousands of mobilized Honduran university students. These students do not see Mr. Zelaya's inadequacies. From their perspective, they only see that their democratic rights have been violated, and this has stirred up their political idealism and a desire to revolt. The next government of Honduras must fully engage students and listen deeply to their concerns. Then, it must respond thoughtfully and swiftly.

THE CIVIL COUP THE WORLD FORGOT

July 19, 2009

Contrary to the popular view that has developed during the past couple of weeks, the "coup" in Honduras did not occur on Sunday, June 28, 2009, but rather on Thursday, June 25. What the world witnessed on Sunday morning in Tegucigalpa was a police action ordered by the Supreme Court of Honduras to put down a coup perpetuated by President Manuel Zelaya three days earlier.

On Thursday morning, Mr. Zelaya gave a rousing speech to hundreds of his supporters at the *Casa Presidencial*. He then urged them to follow him on a special "mission". Mr. Zelaya would not specify the purpose of mission. He simply told people to follow him, as if he were Moses guiding them to the Promised Land. Over the next few hours, Mr. Zelaya led a caravan of buses and other assorted vehicles through the streets of Tegucigalpa toward Toncontín airport. The caravan gradually transformed into a mob.

Wearing his signature white Stetson, Mr. Zelaya and his mob arrived at Hernán Acosta Mejia Air Base (next to Toncontín) that afternoon. They were met at the gate by General Luis Prince, who commanded the base. Mr. Zelaya told General Prince that he had come to retrieve the thousands of boxes of ballots for the scheduled opinion poll that Sunday. The ballots were stored in one of the base's warehouses. Faced with a highly charged mob led by a president demanding entry,

General Prince opened the gate. The mass of people poured onto the base and made their way to the warehouse. They backed up trucks and began loading up the boxes, with President Zelaya right in the middle of all the commotion. It was a surreal environment – something akin to Teddy Roosevelt and his Roughriders charging up San Juan Hill.

Unfortunately, because of the John Wayne western-like drama of it all, the importance of the incident at Hernán Acosta Mejia was lost and quickly overshadowed by the arrest and exile of Mr. Zelaya on June 28. Mr. Zelaya's storming of the base was in fact the start of a "civil coup". The boxes of ballots at the warehouse had been ordered impounded by the Supreme Electoral Tribunal. The Supreme Court had ruled that both the poll set for June 28 and the proposed *cuarta urna* referendum for November 29 were illegal. The military had been ordered to guard the warehouse and block access to the boxes that had been flown in from Venezuela. Mr. Zelaya, backed by the mob, used his position as Commander in Chief of the Armed Forces to intimidate General Prince and gain entry to the base.

As the events unfolded, Mr. Zelaya explained to TV camera crews that what he was doing was simply carrying out the will of the people and that no mere magistrate was going to prevent him from completing his mission. At one point, Mr. Zelaya is filmed standing beside an obviously stunned General Prince, surrounded by the mob. Mr. Zelaya tries to reassure General Prince that he had done right to obey the orders of his Commander in Chief. Mr. Zelaya tells General Prince that everything will be fine because, beginning in 2010, Honduras would be governed by a National Constituent Assembly made up of deputies who would better represent the will of the people. It was clear that Mr. Zelaya already knew the results of both the opinion poll and *la cuarta urna*, suggesting that both processes would be rigged.

By breaking into Hernán Acosta Mejia and retrieving the boxes of ballots from the warehouse, Mr. Zelaya intentionally disobeyed the Supreme Electoral Tribunal. It demonstrated Mr. Zelaya's blatant disregard for the authority of the Judicial branch of government. It was as if he were saying the Judicial branch had no authority over him. It was at that point that many in Honduras became convinced of Mr. Zelaya's commitment to do whatever it took to remain in power. It was then that Mr. Zelaya initiated his civil coup. The Judicial branch was the first victim of the coup. There was a growing fear in Honduras that Mr. Zelaya would then move against the Legislative branch by dissolving Congress (as has been done in Venezuela and Bolivia) and setting up a National Constituent Assembly that he would control. Mr. Zelaya's specific comments on TV about the establishment of the National Constituent Assembly next year indicated that, at least in his mind, this new governing body would become a reality and eventually replace Congress.

Mr. Zelaya should have been arrested and jailed on the evening of June 25 and charged with deliberately disobeying the Supreme Electoral Tribunal after his stunt at Hernán Acosta Mejia. Mr. Zelaya stole materials that had been impounded. The reason that he was not arrested that day is that he had surrounded himself with a mob of hundreds of people – a strategy that was cowardly, at best, and criminal at worst. Mr. Zelaya used his supporters as human shields to prevent security forces from getting close to him. Honduras' military was forced to wait for a more opportune time to arrest Mr. Zelaya when his guard would be down and the risk of a violent confrontation with the mob would be low.

When Honduran soldiers arrested Mr. Zelaya in the early hours of June 28, it was in response to an ongoing three-day-old civil coup perpetuated by Mr. Zelaya against the existing constitutional order. An illegal opinion poll later that day would be used to consolidate Mr. Zelaya's control over the Judicial and Legislative branches. Few people in Honduras were fooled by Mr. Zelaya's intentions because everyone was closely monitoring the events as they unfolded. Unfortunately, the international community tuned in late as the civil coup was ending and instead assumed that it was viewing the start of a military coup. The late arrival by world governments and media has led to a tragic misperception of the truth.

NOTES

How would the US government react if President Obama led a mob through the streets of Washington, DC to Andrews Air Force Base and demanded to be allowed to retrieve documents ordered impounded by the courts? Congress would immediately start impeachment proceedings. The public would be outraged at such audacity and recklessness. Unfortunately, the Honduran Constitution does not provide for the impeachment of a sitting president.

DIPLOMACY IS MORE LIKE CHESS THAN FOOTBALL

July 20, 2009

There is no diabolical conspiracy between Ambassador Hugo Llorens and Mr. Zelaya, as some rumors have suggested. Ambassador Llorens is a career diplomat following a script that has been outlined by US Secretary of State Hillary Clinton, with the approval of President Obama. This is part of a coordinated and extremely sophisticated strategy of trying to isolate Venezuela's Hugo Chávez and his ALBA friends while buying time to calm the situation in Honduras.

During the recent US presidential campaigns of Mrs. Clinton and Mr. Obama, both candidates demonstrated impressive abilities as political strategists. The political machine and strategy that President Obama put together in two short years were masterful. Even Mr. Obama's opponents admire what he did, although they may disagree with him on just about every other issue.

Honduras is too important to the US to allow the situation to be destabilized by Mr. Chávez and ALBA. If Ambassador Llorens were not rubbing Mr. Zelaya's back constantly and reassuring him of US support for his reinstatement, Mel would have nowhere else to go but to Mr. Chávez. At the moment, Mr. Chávez is in check. The talks in Costa Rica are not going extremely well, but they are ongoing. Talks resume on Wednesday.

In the meantime, Mr. Zelaya keeps talking and threatening, but it is talk that is incomprehensible and ultimatums that are empty. So long as the US is perceived as supporting Mr. Zelaya, there is minimum danger that Mr. Chávez would be able to round up support in Latin America for intervention in Honduras. The US has put together its own block of support for a peaceful resolution to the conflict and an eventual "restoration of the constitutional order". This phrase can mean a number of things, not just reinstating Mel. The US block includes Canada, Chile, Mexico, and other countries such as Costa Rica and Panama.

The US' goal is to isolate Mr. Chávez. This is the most effective way to ensure stability in Honduras. Remember, the threat is not Mr. Zelaya, it is Mr. Chávez and ALBA. Think multi-dimensionally. Think about playing chess rather than football.

Lastly, remember that Hugo Llorens is Cuban-American, and he was appointed ambassador to Honduras under the Bush administration. Given his background, Ambassador Llorens would tend to be more conservative than liberal. He is well aware of the dangers of quasi-socialist dictatorships like that of Venezuela, Bolivia, Ecuador, Nicaragua, and of course communist governments like that of Cuba. This man is not naïve. Take a look at his resume and you can see there are relatively few career diplomats with such stellar credentials.

The conflict in Honduras is contained. It could have been much worse, particularly if the US had sided with the interim government from the outset. Mr. Chávez and ALBA would have had a field day. By now, the OAS and most of Latin America and the Caribbean would have been condemning the US position, and the situation would have escalated into a much broader regional one. This would not have been good for the US nor for Honduras, either in the short-term or the long-term.

The US did not create this crisis. This crisis has its roots in Honduras' imbalanced social and economic situation. This crisis was created by Honduran society through apathy, greed, and neglect. Mel is simply a manifestation of the country's deep problems.

NOTES

1. If the Obama administration had supported the coup from the start, Mr. Chávez's influence and popularity in Latin America would have risen because he would have marketed himself as the great moral fighter standing up to the evil Yankees and their old tricks of instigating coups. The US has maintained its legitimacy in the eyes of Latin Americans and has carved out a position for itself as a peacemaker. This is good for Honduras, particularly now that it is facing threats from Venezuela and Nicaragua, and the OAS has been co-opted by the ALBA nations.

2. A US policy in support of the coup would have raised the ire of thousands of Mr. Zelaya's supporters and would have resulted in dozens, perhaps hundreds, of deaths. Because of the traditional negative image of the US in Latin America, the US is potentially an easy pawn for those like Mr. Chávez who wish to stir up public sentiment in their favor. The US did not allow itself to be manipulated this time. Do not forget that when the Honduran drug lord Juan Ramón Matta was captured and taken to the US in the 1980s, Honduran mobs burned the USAID building in Tegucigalpa.

3. The trap was skillfully set, and Mr. Chávez, Mr. Zelaya and all his ALBA friends have fallen into it, almost too easily and ungracefully. Think about it... Latin Americans are asking the US government to intervene directly in the affairs of a Latin

American country? The Obama administration has done the opposite, mildly condemning the coup and imposing soft and temporary sanctions.

4. The Resistance has not been empowered by the official US position toward the coup. In other words, its members are not angry at the US because they perceive the US is on their side. The Hondurans protesting on the streets are angry because they feel they have had something stolen from them. This is what is fueling the Resistance.

5. Some people believe President Obama is a socialist or perhaps even a communist, probably not even an American. But there are no carefully crafted, logical, and convincing arguments explaining why Mr. Obama would want to work with Mr. Chávez to undermine democracy in Honduras. The argument that Mr. Obama and Mr. Chávez are both socialists is not an argument. It is merely easy and simplistic propaganda.

10-POINT REHAB PLAN FOR MEL

July 28, 2009

Dear Mr. Zelaya: you don't know me from Adam, and my advice may not be worth a hill of beans to you... but I will offer you some nonetheless.

1. Fire all of your advisers and strategists. They have served you poorly. Whatever you've been paying them, it's too much. Just look at where you are at the moment.

2. Get out of Ocotal. Unless you're dead serious about starting an insurrection, you're simply isolating yourself from the world, gradually fading from the newspapers, and disappointing many of your followers.

3. Lose the Stetson. President Reagan loved to wear his cowboy hat, but mostly on the ranch. It's hard to take cowboy leaders seriously.

4. Clean up your personal life. There have long been rumors floating around involving ladies who are not your wife and the use of illegal drugs. If there is nothing to these, then I apologize for bringing them up.

5. Stop insulting and belittling people. It doesn't win you any friends or allies.

6. Stop issuing ultimatums you can't back up. It kills your credibility.

7. Accept the fact that you will not be reinstated as president and take any offer of amnesty you can get while you still can. You've already lost your presidency, your party, your reputation, and a large portion of the Honduran people. You are currently a man without a country, unless you wish to risk being imprisoned... in which case you would also lose your freedom.

8. Go back to your ranch in Olancho and reflect for a couple of months about how best to make a positive difference in Honduras and begin to recover much of what you have lost. Get in touch with your spiritual side and lose the ego.

9. Given that you have a significant following among the people of Honduras, consider creating a new political party capable of competing against the Nationalist and Liberal parties. Honduras could use a third party that can represent exclusively the interests of the poor and powerless and truly focus on changing the status quo.

10. Run for a Congressional seat and work to create alliances that can help you reform Honduras' system of government from within.

NOTES

1. Mr. Zelaya continues to hurt himself with silly ultimatums. The man gambled with his risky moves to ally himself with Mr. Chávez and ALBA and pushed efforts that seemed focused on getting himself re-elected. He gambled and lost, and now he is demanding that the world help him retrieve what he lost.

2. Mr. Zelaya and his advisers believe they are the only ones who identify and empathize with the plight of the poor. But given their lifestyles and their arrogance, it appears as if they see themselves as superior. Mr. Zelaya and some of his advisers act more like aristocrats than public servants.

3. If Xiomara Zelaya can march, then why do former ministers not march as well? There are few citizen actions more dignified than a peace march in protest of injustice.

4. Governing involves calculation. Bad governing suggests a series of bad calculations. Mr. Zelaya compiled a series of miscalculations, which caused him to be thrown out of office in a demeaning manner. His failures are largely due to his provocative actions, and thus he has nobody to blame but himself. Mel continues to deny any responsibility for what befell him.

Hugo Chávez: Missing in Action

July 29, 2009

It is no accident that Mr. Chávez (and Mr. Ortega and the OAS) have been uninfluential and powerless in this political crisis. The policy of the Obama administration toward Honduras has been nothing less than brilliant. The US government has managed the crisis in a calm, thoughtful and patient manner. It has looked at the broader picture in Latin America, and has prevented the crisis from escalating.

All of the measures taken by the US have been little more than gentle pinches designed to reassure Mr. Zelaya, Latin America and the international community that it does not support the coup and is trying to "restore the constitutional order". The US is in no great hurry. It is waiting for the elections on November 29. It will be the first to recognize the new president and his administration. This is a classic waiting game. The moves are merely to assuage Mr. Zelaya and let him know that the US is "officially" on his side.

Does anyone seriously believe that the US wants Mr. Zelaya back? The US has important strategic interests in Honduras. It has a military base in the center of the country. It has radar stations. It has a close working relationship with the Honduran military. Honduras is key to drug interdiction efforts. It is key to anti-terrorism efforts. It is key to stemming the tide of illegal immigration into the US.

An Honduras with Mr. Zelaya back in power opens the door to Mr. Chávez and the ALBA nations. It also re-emboldens Mr. Ortega in Nicaragua and the new leftist government in El Salvador under President Mauricio Funes. Were Mr. Zelaya to manage to change the Constitution and be re-elected, does anyone believe that he would not try to kick the US military out of the country? The Obama administration is aware of all of these scenarios. If I can figure this out, then people who have a lot more military and geopolitical experience can too.

NOTES

1. Because of the Obama administration's condemnation of the "hybrid coup" in Honduras, Mr. Chávez is finding it impossible to get much traction in his efforts to portray the US as an accomplice to the action. Mr. Chávez is trying desperately to rouse popular opposition to the US in Latin America, but is failing miserably because Mr. Obama's cool and nuanced approach makes it difficult for Latin Americans to dislike him. Mr. Chávez is not fooled by the Obama administration's lukewarm support of Mr. Zelaya. He knows that the US could apply infinitely more economic, military and political pressure on Honduras. If the US were serious, it would lead a full economic embargo of Honduras and recall its ambassador.

2. The Obama administration recently negotiated an agreement with the government of Colombia to allow US troops to operate within seven military bases in that country. The troops would be involved in anti-drug trafficking activities. The joint US-Honduran air base at Soto Cano does not maintain a large US military presence... only about 600 troops.

What is important to the US is the landing strip and the ability to engage in joint operations with Honduran troops. The US also has radar facilities in Honduras that assist with drug interdiction efforts. Without a US military presence in Honduras, the drug flow from South America into Mexico and then into the US would rise considerably. It does the US little good to increase its presence in Colombia if it does not have Honduras as a midpoint from which to provide logistical support.

ARIAS MEDIATION DOOMED
FROM THE GET-GO

August 24, 2009

The "mediation" process overseen by President Óscar Arias of Costa Rica was a failure in the sense that it has not resolved the conflict between Manuel Zelaya and the interim government of Honduras. In that it kept the parties talking and may have helped calm the situation by creating an illusion of hope so people could justify a respite from the exchange of public accusations and insults, it was a success. It was also a success in that it has isolated Mr. Chávez and his ALBA friends, keeping them in check and unable to stir up too much trouble by taking center stage and using it to spout further polarizing propaganda.

President Arias' failure as a mediator is due less to his skills than to the fact that the process he undertook was a sham from the start. Neither side went into the mediation with a true intent to find common ground. In fact, neither side went into the process with the idea of negotiating. Interim president Roberto Micheletti and Mr. Zelaya never even met face to face. It is doubtful that they could have sat at the same table, much less shaken each other's hand... you know, the sort of stuff that opponents grudgingly do when they sincerely want to find a solution to what separates them.

Prior to the start of the mediation, Mr. Micheletti gave a press conference in Honduras and stated, "We are not going to negotiate anything, we are going to have a dialogue." At about the same time, Mr. Zelaya was quoted in Washington, DC as saying, "It is not about a negotiation, it is about making arrangements for the *golpistas* to leave the country". Well, there you have it. Neither side really ever viewed the talks as negotiations, and President Arias knew this going in.

So, on the one hand, you have to wonder what he was thinking by accepting this seemingly doomed process from the start. On the other hand, you have to give the man a lot of credit for trying, particularly since he knew the whole thing could tarnish his stellar reputation as a peacemaker. No one can take the 1987 Nobel Peace Prize from President Arias, but the star quality of this extremely principled gentleman is much dimmer now. In short, President Arias graciously and willingly took a bullet for the team.

NOTES

1. All talks are good, and so the proposed high-level mission by the OAS consisting of a team of foreign ministers from various countries in the Western Hemisphere should be welcomed in Honduras. What these guys from the OAS do not seem to get, though, is that you cannot continually threaten a government and expel it from your club, and then visit and lay out a set of demands. This is diplomacy at its worst.

2. A mediator does not dictate terms to the parties that are in conflict. A mediator does not show favoritism or make public announcements, particularly when they involve his personal opinions. A mediator does not add to the polarization that already exists. Mr. Arias has displayed no great skills, innovation or out-of-the-box thinking... only one-dimensional ideas for compromises that neither side found appealing. The

problem is that there does not seem to be room for true mediation because neither side has suffered enough. Often, it is only when people have grown exhausted in a conflict that they are willing to give in to a mediated solution in order to stop the pain. Mr. Arias was used from the beginning as a way to calm things down and keep people talking. That alone has been helpful.

3. Xiomara Zelaya's comments yesterday in Tegucigalpa before the commission of visiting foreign ministers from the OAS suggests yet another artificial deadline imposed by Mel. She noted that her husband would agree to sign the "San José Accord" proposed by President Arias so long as the signing takes place in Tegucigalpa no later than September 1. Sounds like a poorly veiled attempt by Mr. Zelaya to gain a well-publicized grand entry into Honduras. The man is nothing if not predictable. He has given too many deadlines and ultimatums to count.

4. One of the central points of the San José Accord calls for putting aside plans for a referendum on whether or not to establish a National Constituent Assembly to review and rewrite the Constitution of Honduras. Mr. Zelaya has now agreed to this condition to his reinstatement as president. This reflects one of the core flaws with all the proposals for settling the political conflict in Honduras. It seems that what the Resistance really wants is not Mr. Zelaya, but rather a National Constituent Assembly that better represents the interests of the people of Honduras. The Resistance wants to change the social and economic status quo. Mr. Zelaya has been little more than a symbol of this goal. In other words, the stakes for Honduran society are much bigger than simply having to deal with Mr. Zelaya's antics for a few months.

A DIGNIFIED IMPASSE?

August 28, 2009

Probably the wealthiest and most influential man in Honduras, Adolfo Facusse, whose family owns most of the textile industry in the country, has said that the business community in Honduras is united in its opposition to any arrangement that would call for the reinstatement of Manuel Zelaya as president. He said that, regardless of the severity of the economic sanctions imposed by the international community, they would not bow down to the pressure.

Yesterday's *La Tribuna* newspaper quoted Mr. Facusse as saying, "We business people have decided that we will not pressure the interim government to accept [a deal that calls for the reinstatement of Mr. Zelaya] just so we can avoid being affected [by the economic sanctions]. We would prefer to eat tortillas and frijoles for a while. It is a matter of dignity."

On the other side of the aisle, there is Berta Cáceres, who is one of the organizers of the National Resistance Front that is leading the demonstrations on the streets in support of Mr. Zelaya's return to power. Ms. Cáceres (no relation to me, by the way) was quoted as saying, "If there is anything that this coup has achieved, it is to unite our entire social movement around an issue that for us is all-important: the return to the constitutional order... but not so that we can stop there, rather so we can continue to move to re-create the Honduran republic."

There you have it. Diametrically opposed positions. The former has little or no interest in changing the status quo in Honduras. The latter's position is all about radically changing the status quo. To both these individuals, the central dividing issue is Mr. Zelaya. To the former, Mel symbolizes a grave threat to normalcy in Honduras. To the latter, Mel symbolizes a vehicle for mobilizing and unifying those who have traditionally been disenfranchised in Honduras... those who have been accustomed to eating a daily diet of tortillas and frijoles.

Neither Mr. Facusse nor Ms. Cáceres appear to have any interest in compromising because each believes those they represent have too much to lose by cutting a deal. Both of them also tend to believe that they have come too far to stop and take a few steps back, so that now it is as much about honor and dignity as anything else. So where does this impasse leave Honduras?

NOTES

1. It is unfortunate to see the peaceful protests by people in support of the reinstatement of Manuel Zelaya turn violent in the streets of Tegucigalpa, because the vast majority of the participants simply wish to march in peace and be heard. The sad part is that it is precisely this violence by the few that may end up drowning out the point the majority is trying to make.

2. The international community underestimates the resolve of the interim government and a large portion of the Honduran population to stand firm against the reinstatement of Mr. Zelaya. Equally, the interim government and much of the population may be underestimating the degree of anger by the sizable portion of the population backing Mel who feel they have been robbed.

3. There is a tendency to ignore or belittle the thousands of people who have consistently protested in the streets of Honduras in favor of Mr. Zelaya. The growth of this movement should not be underestimated. This conflict is no longer solely about Mr. Zelaya, but about how Honduran society is going to find the will and the way to reconcile its differences before it escalates into something bigger and more destabilizing.

HOW 'BOUT REINSTATING MEL
AFTER THE ELECTION?

August 28, 2009

The primary impasse between the interim government of Honduras and the rest of the world is the reinstatement of Manuel Zelaya as president. The interim government's opposition to the reinstatement is also the main reason behind the demonstrations by the Resistance. There are many reasons why the interim government and a very large portion of Honduran society do not accept the reinstatement of Mr. Zelaya, but the primary reason has to do with trust. Many Hondurans simply do not trust Mr. Zelaya to come back and quietly serve out the presidential term of office that ends on January 27, 2010.

There exists a strong and reasonable belief that, if reinstated, Mr. Zelaya would try to force through the creation of a National Constituent Assembly to review and rewrite the Constitution, allowing him to run for a second presidential term, which is prohibited by the Constitution. There is a strong and reasonable belief that Mr. Zelaya would use his powers to incite mobs, as he has done in the past, and use them to manipulate the system to establish *la Constituyente*, try to dissolve the Congress, quickly rewrite the Constitution, run for re-election, rig the election, and remain in power. An easier way might be to simply have *la Constituyente* rewrite the Constitution to allow for an extension of the presidential four-year term, thereby allowing Mr. Zelaya to remain in power and cancel the election altogether.

Granted, this scenario seems almost too fantasy-like to contemplate. But Mr. Zelaya is a fantasy-like character. He is a self-styled *caudillo* and demagogue, and so for him nothing is beyond his reach or too outlandish to consider. A large number of Hondurans fear Mr. Zelaya because he is capable of creating chaos and division in Honduras, and is perfectly willing to do it if it helps him remain in power.

So what is the best way to approach this difficult issue of reinstatement? It is the one issue that continues to isolate Honduras from the world and keeps fueling the demonstrations on the streets. It is the one issue on which there seems to be no desire to compromise. The Micheletti government, with wide support from Honduran society, will not accept Mr. Zelaya's reinstatement. The international community and the Resistance will not back down unless the man is reinstated.

It is possible that the presidential election on November 29 may resolve the impasse, and thus all that is needed is to be patient and wait for election day, hope for a massive turnout of voters, and keep your fingers crossed that it all goes well. This could placate the international community and even some members of the Resistance.

But how would the Micheletti government, Honduran society, the international community, and the Resistance feel about the novel idea of allowing for Mel's reinstatement after November 29? This would help allay fears about the threat of Mr. Zelaya trying to change the rules of the game to stay in power. It would allow the international community to claim a minor, albeit rather hollow, victory. It might also allow Mr. Zelaya to claim a measured victory and save face. A possible reason for Mel being such a pest may have to do as much with his desire to reclaim his honor as it does with any constitutional principle. You have to admit that being awakened in your home at gunpoint and ushered out of your country wearing pajamas is an emasculation from which a man does not readily recover.

Reinstating Mel even after November 29 would require the Micheletti government and much of Honduran society to swallow a heavy dose of pride, but it might be worth it. By then, Honduras would have a newly-elected president, and Mr. Zelaya would be a lame duck president during the Christmas season and the month of January – a lame duck with severely clipped wings, given the conditions that would be imposed as part of the San José Accord proposed by President Arias.

Mr. Zelaya could still create problems by inciting the mobs. But this would likely be no worse than what is already going on in Honduras. The security forces would remain loyal to the Supreme Court and the Congress. If Mr. Zelaya were to again abuse his authority, he could still be arrested by the police and imprisoned. There would be international observers in Honduras to help ensure that Mr. Zelaya would abide by the conditions of the San José Accord. Were Mr. Zelaya to disobey the conditions set forth, he would immediately lose any moral authority he has with the international community.

It would all be a carefully orchestrated waiting game until the next president takes the oath of office on January 27, 2010.

NOTES

1. There is no ambiguity in the position of the interim government, so what is left to negotiate if the primary demand (the reinstatement of Mr. Zelaya) of Mr. Insulza and the OAS is off the table? It seems that Mr. Insulza still believes that the OAS can strong-arm the interim government to acquiesce by threatening heavier sanctions. At this point, nothing would change the minds of those within the interim government, as

they have already been backed into a corner and so they have little to lose by simply waiting.

2. It would be unwise for the interim government not to at least consider all possible options for coming up with an agreement everyone could support. There are dangers associated with any compromise action that gives Mr. Zelaya political power, but there are also dangers to electing a new leader who would not be recognized by the international community. Honduras cannot survive indefinitely isolated from the world. And it cannot survive if the Resistance grows stronger and possibly evolves into a violent movement.

3. The OAS is close to being an irrelevant organization, particularly under the leadership of Mr. Insulza and the influence of Mr. Chávez. It does not matter so much whether the OAS recognizes the results of the elections in November. What matters is that the US government recognizes them. The OAS will eventually follow and re-establish relations with the future government of Honduras.

THE AID GAME

September 3, 2009

For those looking for a story in today's announcement by the US State Department that it will "formally" cut off all non-humanitarian aid to Honduras, they will be disappointed. There is no story. While it may feel as though the US government is piling on the economic sanctions and abandoning Honduras, the reality is much different. The statement by spokesperson Ian Kelly that the US will cut a "wide range of financial assistance" to punish Honduras for the ousting of Manuel Zelaya offers nothing particularly significant.

The assistance that could be affected includes the remaining $135 million of a five-year $215 million Millennium Challenge grant to Honduras signed in 2005 to boost agricultural production and highway construction. An additional $35 million in US aid that had been temporarily suspended soon after June 28 will also be formally cut.

The real story lies not in what the State Department said, but rather what it did not say. It did not tie the termination of aid to a formal determination that the ousting of Mr. Zelaya met the US legal definition of a military coup d'état. Kelly stated, "The Department of State recognizes the complicated nature of the actions which led to the June 28 coup d'état in which Honduras' democratically elected leader, President Zelaya, was removed from office".

Had the State Department made a formal determination that the ousting of Mr. Zelaya met the US's legal definition of a military coup d'état, it would have triggered legislation passed by Congress forcing the Obama administration to cut off aid to Honduras. By not triggering this legislation, the State Department maintains a high degree of independence and thus flexibility in its ability to conduct foreign policy toward Honduras. There is a lot of nuance here, which is in line with President Obama's leadership style.

Thus, in this case the US has condemned the "coup" in Honduras and is willing to impose severe economic sanctions, but it is not willing to legally define it as a coup for reasons that have more to do with pragmatism than principle.

Even the severity of the economic sanctions is not at all what it seems. First of all, it's not clear whether any of the roughly $170 million in terminated aid was even scheduled to be disbursed during the next few months. Furthermore, the termination of that aid is conditional. Mr. Kelly stated that restoring aid will depend on "a return to democratic, constitutional governance in Honduras". Kelly continued, "[The November] election must be undertaken in a free, fair and transparent manner, it must also be free of taint and open to all Hondurans to exercise their democratic franchise". The wording suggests that the US is looking to the elections as a legitimate way to resolve this conflict.

For weeks Secretary of State Clinton has been stressing the importance of "re-establishing the constitutional order" in Honduras. This may or may not include the reinstatement of Mr. Zelaya as president. The US appears to be more interested in a "free, fair and transparent" process.

So the good news for Honduras is two-fold. The US government is keeping an open mind about the elections on November 29, which suggests that it dearly wants to recognize the results of the elections. And if all goes well (which depends on the interim government and people of Honduras), then all the aid that was cut will be restored.

It may be purely coincidental, but last week the International Monetary Fund (IMF) disbursed $150 million to the Micheletti government, and it plans to disburse another $13.8 million on September 9. The total of $163.8 million would nearly make up for the approximately $170 million in US aid that may be affected by the State Department's announcement today.

NOTES

1. It is important to understand that the aid cuts announced by the State Department will have virtually no impact on the poor in Honduras. It is a relatively small amount of money, and all of it will likely be restored within a few months. It is possible that most, if not all, of that money was not even scheduled to be disbursed any time soon. And much of it was destined for highway construction and agricultural production programs (not humanitarian projects) that do not immediately benefit the poor in Honduras. In fact, much of the foreign aid that is channeled through the Honduran government does not benefit the poor. The money gets lost in the pipeline, which is why Honduras remains the fourth poorest country in the Western Hemisphere. Most foreign aid programs simply aggravate income inequality in countries like Honduras that do not have well educated populations that know how to take full advantage of government aid programs.

2. In private, both President Obama and Secretary of State Clinton must be happy to be rid of Mr. Zelaya, but it would be horrendous geopolitics to reveal this in public. So long as there is relative calm in Honduras and the elections proceed in a peaceful, organized, transparent and fair manner, then there is no reason for the US not to be the first to recognize the results of the elections.

3. Honduras has suffered emotionally from feeling that the entire world has turned against it. From a financial standpoint, the real damage to Honduras has been caused by the 80 percent drop in tourism. That would have happened regardless of US policy. At some point, Hondurans will have to accept full responsibility for the failures of their society. The US is a convenient scapegoat.

DEAR ELVIN AND PEPE

September 3, 2009

Dear Elvin and Pepe: You have three months to campaign for the office of President of Honduras. The time has come to demonstrate that you are truly different kinds of leaders. Consider not spending your money on self-promoting colorful advertisements and radio and TV spots with silly slogans. Consider not promising a lot of stuff you will never be able to deliver.

Entertain the thought of not attacking each other or claiming that others are attacking you. Do not portend to be the saviors of Honduras. Each of you is a guy... nothing more, nothing less. Do not just go around giving speeches at functions at hotels and auditoriums filled with adoring, flag-waving fans who will cheer you regardless of what you say.

Forget all of that, and do something really radical and deeply human. Go visit with the poorest of the poor in Honduras. Go listen to them. Listen. Go live their daily lives with them. Go be with them every day until November 29. You will gain empathy, and you will be transformed. And then maybe you will become the kind of leader that Honduras needs.

Start with the municipal garbage dump outside of Tegucigalpa, on the road to Olancho. Let me know if you need directions and personal introductions to the hundreds of men, women and children who live and work there, and I'll find the right person to guide you.

NOTES

1. When candidates start using the word "victory" in their speeches and use salutes of allegiance to the party... well then, the prospects for true national reconciliation start to fade quickly.

2. What is it about politicians that they cannot understand the inherent hypocrisy of criticizing their opponents for being partisan while proceeding to act in a partisan manner themselves? Partisan means believing only you, your candidate, and your party hold the answers to your country's problems. Being non-partisan means that you do not care which candidate or party wins so long as the ideas and proposals for resolving the problems are good and valid. It is time to take off the colors.

3. Allegiances to colors, logos, flags, individuals, and geographic boundaries are tribalistic, and thus limit the ability or even willingness to find common ground. These loyalties to things artificial fuel the perception of "us" versus "them", which too often unnecessarily maximizes our differences while minimizing our similarities.

4. Salutes of allegiance, fist pumping, victory signs, and flag waving are traditionally meant to unite and energize one's tribe... to the exclusion of the other tribes. Is this really what we want of our politicians in Honduras at this moment in history?

THE GREATER RIFT

October 4, 2009

Mr. Zelaya and the Micheletti government are much farther apart than is being reported by the press and by the various foreign diplomats and politicians visiting Honduras. Mr. Zelaya and his supporters are saying that they will not proceed with their plans to set up a National Constituent Assembly this year if Mr. Zelaya is reinstated as president. This is being sold as some sort of concession.

However, the idea of a National Constituent Assembly was never supposed to be a done deal. While it may have been in Mr. Zelaya's plans, officially the setting up of this body was to be based on the results of *la cuarta urna* referendum, which itself was also never a given. The so-called *encuesta* (opinion poll) that was to have determined whether or not to set up *la cuarta urna* on November 29 was never held due to Mr. Zelaya's ousting.

So why has the idea of a National Constituent Assembly now suddenly emerged as a concession? Besides, even Mr. Zelaya has always stated that, in the event (assuming no manipulation) the results of *la cuarta urna* supported the creation of a National Constituent Assembly, the process would not take place until the next presidential term which begins on January 27, 2010. So what is it that Mr. Zelaya is conceding by agreeing to what he has always officially supported in the first place?

While he is living in the Brazilian embassy in Tegucigalpa with his estranged wife and about 80 of his supporters (most of whom have been sleeping on the floor for the past two weeks) and is dependent on the goodwill of the interim government and the UN for access to food, water, communication, and clean clothes, Mr. Zelaya continues to act as if he is the man in command of the situation. He continues to dictate the terms and conditions of any dialogue with those who oppose him, as if he is the one with unlimited time, patience, and comfort.

Mr. Zelaya's first and foremost condition is that he be reinstated as president of Honduras. Once he is in power again (although he would lack any real power, as no institution of government would recognize his authority), he would graciously offer to postpone the establishment of a National Constituent Assembly. That's it? That's his bargaining position?

Three months after Mr. Zelaya's ousting, the opposing sides are as far apart as they have ever been. The difference is that everyone is exhausted from talking at each other and the country is just a little bit poorer and more defaced with graffiti. The interim government has consolidated its power and has endured the threats and pressures from the international community, while organizations such as the OAS and numerous regional governments (Venezuela, Nicaragua and Brazil) and leaders (Chávez , Ortega, Lula and Arias) have been discredited or weakened.

Mr. Zelaya, meanwhile, has exposed himself countless times as an individual who has a tendency to be reckless and politically inept. His power has been steadily diminished by a series of miscalculations, disappointments, and generally poor or non–existent planning. Time is not in his favor, as world events move forward and leave him behind mindlessly repeating the same old canned speeches, calls to insurrection, and concessions that are not really concessions.

NOTES

1. It is important to try and empathize with the people who are demonstrating on the streets. The people are within their rights to demonstrate peacefully as long as they wish, and it appears as if they could continue for some time. The length of these demonstrations may depend on when the candidates will awaken from their slumber and come up with a visionary plan of action for national reconciliation that can attract the interest of the Resistance. The plan cannot include the reinstatement of Mr. Zelaya, but it might include convening a National Constituent Assembly to review the Constitution. That would be ironic.

2. The Resistance has evolved to where it is less concerned about Mr. Zelaya and Mr. Micheletti than the establishment of a National Constituent Assembly to better represent the interests of the people (primarily the poor). If it is true that the Resistance on the streets of Honduras is morphing into something more ominous than what is being reported in news stories, then this political crisis may only be in the early stages.

3. There is nothing that guarantees that a National Constituent Assembly will be any less corrupt or incompetent than the Congress. What is the point of creating another institution? Why not find a way to reform the institution of Congress? One of the things that continually holds Honduras back is that its people are always looking for that quick fix to all their problems.

4. Revolutionary changes that are pushed through by coercion and confrontation usually do not work, and those who suffer the most from these traumatic jolts to society always end up being the poor.

5. Interim president Micheletti miscalculated when he issued the decree suspending civil liberties in Honduras. The decree will soon be lifted, given that it can only further damage Honduras' image around the world and will do nothing to encourage recognition of the results of the elections on November 29. Mr. Micheletti overreacted to Mr. Zelaya's most recent call for insurrection. The Brazilian Congressional representatives who met with Mel a couple of days ago cautioned him to tone down his language, as did visiting US government officials. There is a great deal of fear and mistrust on both sides, and this is opening the way for dangerous miscalculations.

6. Mr. Zelaya's hasty return to Tegucigalpa has transformed the political crisis in Honduras into an internal matter. No longer is Mel traveling up and down the Western Hemisphere giving speeches, meeting with government leaders, and posing for photos. This is no longer an international story, and so Mel has brilliantly deprived himself of the relatively little leverage (international pressure created by international exposure) he had following his overthrow.

IRONIES OF A WORLD CUP CLINCHER

October 15, 2009

There is a degree of irony in that the last and only time Honduras made it to the World Cup (in 1982) was the year that the country's Constitution was written. The Constitution was completed on January 11, 1982 and went into effect shortly afterward on January 20. The '82 World Cup was held in Spain that summer, beginning on June 13 and ending with Italy's 3-1 win over Germany on July 11.

Now... 27 years later, the second time Honduras qualifies for a World Cup, it occurs during a year marked by political turmoil fueled by deposed president Manuel Zelaya's efforts to push through a process to rewrite that same Constitution. Fascinating coincidence.

It is also ironic that the first Honduran player to score a goal in the '82 World Cup was a guy named "Zelaya". Héctor Zelaya scored his famous goal against the Spanish national team on June 16, 1982. While Zelaya is a common last name in Honduras, it's still an interesting coincidence.

There is further irony in that the team Honduras has edged out for passage to the World Cup in South Africa next year is Costa Rica... the country to which Mr. Zelaya was flown to immediately after his arrest by the Honduran Armed Forces on June 28. San José, Costa Rica was also the site of two rounds of talks in July between representatives of the Micheletti government and Mr. Zelaya. The talks were mediated by Costa

Rica's president, Óscar Arias, who subsequently went on to win the ire of many Hondurans by trying to impose a deal that nobody seemed interested in signing and, further, by referring to the Honduran Constitution as the world's worst.

So now the Costa Rican national team must go off and play a pretty good team from Uruguay in a playoff match to determine the wild card entry from the Americas to the 2010 World Cup. Honduras' path to South Africa is clear. A little poetic justice perhaps?

Finally, it's always wonderful to see a little payback. Throughout the political crisis during the past three and a half months, the United States has been a pain in the neck for Honduras. In response to the ousting of Mr. Zelaya, the US State Department has been extremely critical of Honduras and has tried to pressure the country's interim government by cutting military assistance, terminating more than $30 million in economic aid, and suspending the issuing of visas to Honduran citizens. The Obama administration has insinuated that it might even entertain the idea of not recognizing the results of the presidential election on November 29.

Many in Honduras have felt betrayed by the US and perplexed as to why a traditional friend and ally should be so threatening. Enter Jonathan Bornstein. With only 20 seconds to play in the Costa Rica-US match, Costa Rica is leading 2-1. A win by Costa Rica automatically sends the Costa Rican team to the World Cup. A tie or a loss opens the door for Honduras. Bornstein scores. The game ends 2-2. Honduras proceeds to the World Cup.

It may take a while for Honduras to fully forgive the US for its perceived lack of support during the political crisis. But the handsome Mr. Bornstein is suddenly an Honduran hero, and there are more than a fair share of "thank you USA" signs showing up in street celebrations throughout Honduras. Not a bad start. By the way, it's impossible not to notice that both

Bornstein's score and the goal by Carlos Pavón that lifted Honduras over El Salvador were both beautiful headers set up by assists from the right side of the field.

The spirit of sport (in the case of Honduras, *futbol*) is wonderful. Unlike the spirits of politics and religion, it is uncomplicated. The results are clear. It may well end up accomplishing what politicians, diplomats and bureaucrats have failed to do... unite the people of Honduras, at least for a few precious months. Sure would be great if all nations could settle their conflicts on a green field with a leather ball.

PREVENTIVE WAR

October 21, 2009

One of the tenets of the so-called "Bush Doctrine" was the controversial policy of "preventive war", which held that the United States should depose foreign regimes that represented a potential or perceived threat to the security of the United States. It is what supposedly justified the US invasion of Iraq. The overthrow of Mr. Zelaya can be thought of in terms of this tenet.

The overthrow was motivated by a fear that Mr. Zelaya was trying to consolidate power and eventually seek to change the political system in Honduras so he could position himself to remain in power for a very long time... much in the same way Hugo Chávez has done in Venezuela and Daniel Ortega is now doing in Nicaragua, and of course Mr. Castro has done in Cuba for the past half century.   Populists or nationalists like Mr. Zelaya and these other men – along with others throughout history like Mussolini, Hitler, Qaddafi, and Hussein – initially start out with good intentions (or not), but they tend to become corrupted by their ego's unquenchable thirst for power and dominance. The danger is that they are apt to frame everything they do in the context of what is best for the people ("El Pueblo"), and thus everything they do is held up as justified and perhaps sacred, even if it means sacrificing the rights, freedoms, and physical welfare of some or many within a society.

Had Mr. Zelaya been thinking and acting alone, it is unlikely that the powers that be in Honduras would have moved against him. The fact that Mr. Zelaya had become enamored with and beholden to Mr. Chávez and his associates in Bolivia, Ecuador, and Nicaragua made him infinitely more threatening than he would have been otherwise.

Arguing about whether or not Mr. Zelaya's removal from power was legal or illegal is a useless exercise. It is irrelevant to argue legalities when a nation or a segment of society feels threatened and fears what is happening or what may happen in the future if some sort of action is not taken. The idea is that you'd better strike before your enemy strikes. Ultimately, it is up to the individual, group of individuals, or nation that strikes first to endure the consequences of acting or waiting.

The idea of prevention was considered by those within the upper echelon of the Bush administration when it was decided that the US should launch its invasion of Iraq. Similarly, prevention may have been on the minds of the fifteen judges of Honduras' Supreme Court when they unanimously voted to arrest President Zelaya. Both the US military intervention in Iraq and the removal of Mr. Zelaya by the Honduran military are controversial from moral and legal standpoints. Good and reasonable people can argue in defense of or in opposition to each action.

The US government understands the tenet of preventive war. Its policymakers in the State Department fully understand the motivation behind the removal of Mr. Zelaya, and they may well sympathize with it. But they cannot support it because they realize it would set a dangerous precedent that might give the green light to opposing political factions in other countries who could be waiting for an excuse to move against freely elected democratic leaders favorable to the US. Giving tacit approval to overthrow leaders through military force sets a precedent that could trigger the installation of dictatorial regimes hostile to the US.

The US government may feel that it is geopolitically safer and more advantageous to the US, overall, to oppose a change of government that at least appears to occur outside the constitutional norms... even if such a change might be beneficial to a country in the short-term and possibly the long-term.

NOTES

Whether Mel is or is not Hugo Chávez is not the point. The point is whether a sizeable portion of the Honduran population believes that he is a follower of Mr. Chávez. The perception is that President Zelaya intended to copy the Venezuelan model – something that many Hondurans believe would be a disaster for the country.

MEL'S ASSUMPTIONS

November 4, 2009

If you read through the provisions of the Tegucigalpa-San José Accord, nowhere does the agreement specify that the Honduran Congress must vote to reinstate Manuel Zelaya as president of Honduras. It simply says that the authority to do so will be given to Congress. The agreement places no conditions on Congress, and it does not set a deadline by which Congress should act. Given all of this, it is puzzling to hear that Mr. Zelaya is now saying that if Congress does not vote to reinstate him by Thursday, November 5, then he will consider the agreement to be null and void. It seems as if Mr. Zelaya is reading a different version of the agreement than has been made available to the public.

So the question is, "What has led Mr. Zelaya to interpret things the way he has?" More to the point, "What makes Mr. Zelaya believe that he has anywhere close to the number of votes he needs in Congress?" He can count the votes in Congress as well as anyone else and thus, absent some sort of "closet deal" that would transfer dozens of unexpected Liberal and Nationalist party votes to his side, he should easily be able to conclude that his chances of winning are slim to none.

Mr. Zelaya probably has a few more than 20 votes within his own Liberal party. There are a total of 62 Liberal members of Congress. Mr. Zelaya can count on five votes from the Democratic Unification (UD) Party and one from the Christian

Democracy (DC) Party. Is there a member of the opposition Nationalist Party who would chose to side with Mr. Zelaya? The leader of the Nationalist Party, Porfirio Lobo, has categorically denied reports that he has made a deal to sway the other 54 Nationalist members of Congress to vote for Mr. Zelaya.

Mr. Zelaya requires at least 65 of the total 128 Congressional votes to be restored to power. At the moment, he has less than 30, and there exists no groundswell of support for Mr. Zelaya within the Congress. Mr. Zelaya has used up much if not most of his political capital during the past four months as a result of his erratic behavior, at times insulting language, efforts to incite insurrection, and repeated political miscalculations. It is difficult to see the attraction to a member of Congress of voting to reinstate Mr. Zelaya unless that member maintains a personal loyalty to him, experiences remorse for having initially backed his ousting, or feels pressured in some way.

The key to understanding Mr. Zelaya's reasoning may lie in his repeated references to the provision in the Tegucigalpa-San José Accord that calls for the establishment of a Government of Unity and National Reconciliation by November 5. He regularly links the setting up of the reconciliation government with his reinstatement. In fact, Mr. Zelaya holds out his reinstatement as a prerequisite for this new government, which suggests that he has been working under the assumption that the agreement his negotiators signed on October 30 calls for a Government of Unity and National Reconciliation headed by a President Manuel Zelaya.

Given this assumption by Mr. Zelaya, of course it follows that Congress must vote to reinstate him sometime on Friday morning or early afternoon. Otherwise, the provision calling for a reconciliation government could not be implemented on time or at all, and therefore the agreement would be broken.

Therein lies one of the central problems with the agreement... its provisions are not specific enough, and so each side has an overabundance of latitude to interpret them as they wish, based on their own assumptions.

To be fair to the six individuals who negotiated the Tegucigalpa-San José Accord, they were under so much pressure to make a deal that it was not feasible to include too many logistical details. Had the negotiators opted to pack the agreement with timelines and conditions, the talks would have stalled and there would have been no deal.

The negotiators sidestepped the problem of the agreement being too general by including a provision to set up a Verification Commission to oversee the implementation of the agreement. Perhaps, for the sake of expediency, the negotiators chose to let the four-member Verification Commission figure out the specifics. That commission met for the first time on Tuesday and consists of Arturo Corrales representing the Micheletti government, Jorge Arturo Reina representing Mr. Zelaya, the former president of Chile, Ricardo Lagos, and US Secretary of Labor Hilda Solis.

NOTES

1. Two proposals that have been submitted to Mr. Zelaya as part of the *Diálogo Guaymuras* call for: 1) the Supreme Court to decide on the reinstatement of Mr. Zelaya as president and the Congress to authorize the decision, or 2) the Supreme Court and the Congress to jointly decide on Mr. Zelaya's reinstatement. Mr. Zelaya has rejected both proposals. Instead, he has renewed his calls on the OAS and the UN to pressure the interim government to reinstate him. The question Mr. Zelaya has not answered (and perhaps it hasn't been asked) is, "How would you go about governing Honduras

without the trust or respect of either the Judicial or Legislative branches?" Would specially appointed committees within OAS and the UN serve as de facto governing branches of the Honduran government until January 27, 2010?

2. When the Honduran Congress votes against reinstating Mr. Zelaya as president, the US government will feign disappointment, but it's hard to believe that the State Department ever really thought the Tegucigalpa-San José Accord would favor Mr. Zelaya. The US government can count votes as well as anyone, and a sufficient number of votes in favor of Mr. Zelaya do not exist. It is possible that Mr. Zelaya signed the agreement because he was pressured in ways that will never be known. He could also have been persuaded that he stood a good chance of winning in Congress – a reasonable possibility, given Mr. Zelaya's self-infatuation.

A Reconciliation Government Without Mel

November 6, 2009

Can you really have a Government of Unity and National Reconciliation in Honduras when those with whom you seek unity and reconciliation are not included? Deposed president Manuel Zelaya was asked by the Micheletti government to submit a list of ten people whom he would like to nominate to be a part of the transitional government being established under the terms of the Tegucigalpa-San José Accord. Mr. Zelaya has refused to nominate anyone until Congress votes to reinstate him as president. Thus, neither he nor any of his supporters will be represented in the new government, which will serve until January 27, 2010 when the next president is inaugurated

Although Mr. Zelaya did not submit his ten names in time to meet yesterday's deadline for formation of the reconciliation government, he is being given additional time to consider candidates by the Micheletti government. The Minister of the Presidency, Rafael Pineda Ponce said, "We will continue waiting [for Mr. Zelaya's list] if that is what he wishes."

Thus far, the names of 24 nominees to fill positions within the reconciliation government have been submitted. These individuals are from all sectors of Honduras, including civil society. Several parties will be represented, including the Liberal and Nationalist parties, as well as smaller parties such as the Innovation and Social Democrat Unity (PINU–SD) and Christian Democracy (DC) parties.

Names submitted by the PINU-SD include Gaspar Vallecillo, Maricela Bustillo, Roberto Leiva, Liliana Antonia Medina, Mario Alfredo Moya, Iveth Hernández, Jorge Salgado, Esperanza Moreno, German Leitzelar Hernández and Miguel Angel Cálix. The DC nominees include Roberto Vallejo, Liliana Izaguirre, Julio Larios, Lucy Navarrete, Jorge Machado, Santiago Reyes, Alejandro Amaya, Marco Antonio Reyes and Humberto Sánchez.

At least six of the current members of Mr. Micheletti's cabinet will remain in place. These are Mr. Ponce; Carlos López Contreras, Minister of Foreign Relations; Gabriela Núñez, Minister of Finance; Héctor Hernández Amador, Minister of Agriculture and Livestock; Adolfo Lionel Sevilla, Minister of Defense; and Jorge Rodas Gamero, Minister of Security.

On Thursday evening, ministers and other officials within interim president Robert Micheletti's cabinet resigned from their posts to allow for their replacements under the Government of Unity and National Reconciliation. While this move will change the appearance of the Honduran government, it leaves unanswered the question of what role Mr. Zelaya and his supporters will play in the new administration. If so, then also left unanswered is how the process of unity and reconciliation can move forward.

MISREADING NUANCED DIPLOMACY

November 13, 2009

Since the signing of the Tegucigalpa-San José Accord on October 30 by representatives of interim president Roberto Micheletti and deposed president Manuel Zelaya, three US State Department officials have stated clearly that the US will support the Honduran national elections scheduled for November 29 and recognize their results regardless of whether Mr. Zelaya is reinstated as president. First in line was Assistant Secretary of State for Western Hemisphere Affairs, Thomas Shannon.

In an interview with CNN on November 3, Mr. Shannon revealed that, although the US government still condemned the ousting of Mr. Zelaya and supported his reinstatement, it would respect the outcome of a vote on this issue by Honduras' Congress. The implication was that the Obama administration would not place any conditions on its support for the elections. It seemed a reasonable position to take, given that the Tegucigalpa-San José Accord placed no conditions or even timetables on the vote by Congress.

Then came US Ambassador to Honduras, Hugo Llorens, who a few days after the CNN interview, reaffirmed Mr. Shannon's position. Finally, this past week, Deputy Assistant Secretary of State for Western Hemisphere Affairs, Craig Kelly, reiterated the same position.

By opting to publicly announce to the world that the US government is now committed to the upcoming elections and, even more, sees them as the key to resolving the political crisis in Honduras, State Department officials have in one fell swoop eliminated the only leverage that Mr. Zelaya possessed to at least mildly influence the Micheletti administration and Congress to being more amenable to his demand to be reinstated.

Mr. Zelaya has discovered that the support he thought he had from the US has suddenly vanished. He must be asking himself, "Man, what in the heck just happened?" It is possible that Mr. Zelaya thoroughly misread and overestimated the Obama administration's commitment to him from the very beginning.

The record of remarks from State Department officials and spokespersons since July has consistently been one of support for the re-establishment of the constitutional order in Honduras. Occasionally, the line varies a bit to include something along the lines of, "We believe Mr. Zelaya should be returned to power", but that version is recited quickly and rather awkwardly, and almost never in the same sentence as comments related to the elections. The phrase "re-establishing the constitutional order" is practiced much more often, and it is obvious that they are infinitely more comfortable to the official uttering them.

Mr. Zelaya chose to interpret the State Department's position in the manner that sounded most attractive to him, instead of trying to read between the lines for what was being subtly conveyed. He should have started to catch on when State Department spokespersons began saying things like, "We do not support any one individual, but rather the return to democratic rule in Honduras".

As to the matter of the elections, the US government has never explicitly come out and stated that it would not recognize

MARCO CÁCERES DI IORIO

their results unless Mr. Zelaya was reinstated. What State Department officials and spokespersons have said repeatedly is that it would be difficult for the US to recognize the elections given "existing conditions" in Honduras out of concern that the process could not be undertaken in a transparent, fair, and inclusive manner. Existing conditions could mean anything from riots in the streets to repression of the media. It could also be taken to mean Mr. Zelaya being out of power.

The problem for Mr. Zelaya has been his inability to grasp both the tone and content of the nuanced language that is used by the State Department under the Obama administration. It does not help that Mr. Zelaya does not speak fluent English, so he is bound to miss things.

Technically, the US has been consistent in its policy toward Honduras. Its position has evolved, but it has not been reversed, as Mr. Zelaya now seems to believe. The evolution has occurred because the political situation in Honduras has superficially changed over the past two weeks, notably the signing of the Tegucigalpa-San José Accord – an agreement that, although vaguely and poorly crafted from the standpoint of a conflict resolution plan, has allowed the US government to claim a foreign policy victory. It is still unclear what motivated Mr. Zelaya to sign a deal so detrimental to his cause.

By getting the opposing sides to come together and work out their differences and then sign a piece of paper, the US government can congratulate itself and say that it has done its part, and that now the time has come for Hondurans to resolve among themselves the final loose ends of their family quarrel.

Mr. Zelaya has every right to feel that he has been tricked. His position is vastly weaker than it was two weeks ago. He can no longer count on the weight of the US government to try and influence events. And those such as Venezuela's Hugo Chávez and José Miguel Insulza of the OAS, who have more sincerely backed Mr. Zelaya, have been made irrelevant either by their own missteps or by US diplomatic maneuvering. But Mr. Zelaya is a grown man and a veteran politician, so he has nobody to blame but himself.

NOTES

1. One of the strangest things about Mr. Zelaya is that his steady stream of political miscalculations always seem to place him in positions of weakness that also weaken those who try to help him and those whom he is supposedly trying to help. In what appears to be a narcissistic disassociation from reality, he adamantly believes that he can dictate terms and conditions to all those who oppose him, continue to consolidate power, and grow relatively stronger with the passing of time.

2. It is nice to think that had the US government taken the position of supporting Honduran democracy by not condemning the overthrow of Mr. Zelaya and letting Honduras handle the situation by itself everything would have turned out just fine, but this would not have been the case. It required US backdoor diplomacy and strategizing to come up with an agreement that clearly was in the Micheletti government's favor and isolated Mr. Zelaya and his friends. Honduras is a small country. It needs the US as a friend and ally. Sometimes when there are bullies lurking, friends and allies must act in ways that do not at first seem beneficial to those they are trying to help.

3. In an article in today's *Washington Post* titled, "Honduras Accord is On Verge of Collapse", Mr. Zelaya was quoted as saying of the US government, "Their priorities were my reinstatement." Referring to the US' stated commitment to support the upcoming elections regardless of whether Mr. Zelaya is reinstated, Mr. Zelaya said, "This is a very dangerous change of foreign policy for the United States." Therein lies the core of Mr. Zelaya's misunderstanding. The priority for the US has never been the reinstatement of Mr. Zelaya. It has consistently been about "re-establishing the constitutional order". Mr. Zelaya has assumed that this implies his reinstatement. There has been no significant change in US policy. The difference is that now the elections are closer, and the game has become much less nuanced.

PLAYING AT UNITY AND RECONCILIATION

November 13, 2009

The current difficulty in implementing the "Government of Unity and National Reconciliation" for Honduras first proposed by Costa Rican president Óscar Arias as part of the San José Accord negotiated in July, and subsequently incorporated into the *Diálogo Guaymuras* and the Tegucigalpa-San José Accord signed by representatives of the Micheletti government and Mr. Zelaya on October 30, is that not enough thought has been given to the words "unity" and "reconciliation". It is as if whoever came up with the idea of incorporating these words into the title of what is envisioned as a transitional power-sharing government felt the words would automatically add strength and legitimacy to the new institution, making it palatable to all sides involved in the political crisis.

The problem is that unity and reconciliation do not just happen; they are delicate processes that take time, particularly in a country like Honduras where a society has been polarized by a controversial and provocative president and traumatized by his forceful overthrow. The reality is that, as wonderful as it would be to have unity and reconciliation in Honduras, the mood of the country is not conducive to these processes. Honduran society is tired of the relative uncertainty and instability that it has been living with for the past four-and-a-half months, but there is no authentic desire or will to put aside differences and humbly ask for and grant forgiveness, and then cheerfully move on.

When individuals truly seek unity and reconciliation, the reasonable and enlightened thing that happens is that they meet face to face and say something like, "Hey, I'm sorry for the trouble and pain that I've caused you. Please forgive me." What also happens is that each person displays a willingness to listen intently to the other so that understanding and empathy can take hold. Honduras is not close to seeing this kind of meeting between Roberto Micheletti and Manuel Zelaya, or between their supporters.

Sadly, people all too often refer to each other as *golpistas* or *comunistas* – and these are the more polite epithets. If you happen to oppose Mr. Zelaya, you are naturally a *golpista*, an enemy of democracy. If you happen to support Mr. Zelaya, you must of course be a *comunista* (or at least a socialist), or at minimum, blind. The intention of this act of labeling or painting with a broad stroke is to diminish the person who does not happen to agree with your perspective of what has happened. In other words, only you are the holder of the truth.

Until we begin to accept that each person only grasps pieces of the truth of the events leading up to June 28 and everything that has happened since that day, we will not be ready to move toward unity and reconciliation in Honduras. We must also realize that unity and reconciliation are dynamic processes that must be built up by taking baby steps (like putting aside the labels) consistently over a period of time.

It was a nice thought to attach feel-good words like "unity" and "reconciliation" to a temporary government theoretically designed to resolve the complex political issues that divide Hondurans. But it was premature. The hard work is still before us.

NOTES

Regardless of what happens to Mel Zelaya, Honduran society and its political leaders should start to prepare themselves for the possibility of entertaining some radical social and economic changes in Honduras. If the Resistance is not placated, distracted, or soothed by the elections, and it continues to grow and spread after November 29, then whatever government is in power is going to face the unpleasant prospect of feeling forced to become more repressive. Such a scenario would not bode well for stability in Honduras. There needs to be an authentic movement within the government in partnership with the business sector, civil society, and the Resistance to form a Government of National Reconciliation (without Mr. Zelaya) that would seek to develop a consensus on how to govern Honduras in a way that better represents the interests of the majority of Hondurans.

MEL'S LETTER TO OBAMA

November 17, 2009

When you write a letter to someone, the assumption is that you intend for that person to read your letter. If Manuel Zelaya is expecting President Obama to read his recent rambling, grammatically imperfect, five-page letter written in Spanish, he is in for a disappointment. The letter, dated November 14, is filled with flowery words and poorly-constructed sentences that force you to re-read them several times in order to get the point or even understand the basic meaning behind the thoughts. In several paragraphs, Mr. Zelaya displays a powerful disdain for the use of periods, causing the reader to quickly get lost in a maze of commas. He displays an annoying affection for the use of bolding and underlining to stress that which he considers vital... almost as if Mr. Zelaya is aware that he is lulling you to sleep with his excessive recounting of historical events and wishes to snap you out of your dazed state.

The biggest problem with Mel's letter is quite simply its length. One of the first lessons a legislative aide on Capitol Hill learns is that memos for Members of Congress should never exceed one page because politicians are so busy that they do not have the time or inclination to read anything longer. It is the same advice given to college students when they compose their resumes. If it can't be said in one page, you will fail to get the attention of the intended reader. Long-windedness is not a positive attribute, but rather an indication of egocentrism, a disorganized mind, and emotional insecurities. Being concise is usually the better way to go because it shows that you have clear thoughts that can be expressed in precise sentences that do not need to be repeated or decorated with ornaments.

A more minor problem is the fact that Mel's letter was written in Spanish. Mr. Zelaya does not have command of the English language. He sees himself as the President of Honduras and feels that it is proper form to write in the language of his country, and that may be so. However, Mr. Zelaya finds himself in a difficult and increasingly isolated position. He is not sitting in a position of strength or authority. So the assumption is that he very much wants and needs President Obama to listen to him and respond quickly. The final sentence in Mr. Zelaya's letter includes, "I await your prompt response". Consequently, you would think Mr. Zelaya would have taken the time to have someone translate his letter into flawless English in order to avoid having a staffer at the White House or State Department be assigned the task of translating it and perhaps risk his letter getting lost in the shuffle of everyday business in Washington.

And finally, it is worth noting the importance of timing when writing such a letter. It would not be advisable, for example, to write an urgent letter to someone who is preparing for or returning from a trip. It would be especially unwise to write an urgent letter to someone who is already off traveling on vacation or on a business trip. You just won't get their attention. Last week, President Obama left on an eight-day trek of Asia. He made stops in Japan and Singapore, where he attended the Asia-Pacific Economic Cooperation summit and the Association of Southeast Asian Nations economic forum. This week, he is in China meeting with President Hu Jintao and other Chinese leaders to discuss a range of issues, including US-China trade relations and North Korea's nuclear activities. President Obama's final stop before returning to the US on Friday will be South Korea where he will meet with President Lee Myung-bak and deliver a speech to US troops at Osan Air Base.

It is doubtful that President Obama will review Mr. Zelaya's letter this week, much less get around to dictating a response. With such a slight chance of Mr. Zelaya's letter making President Obama's top ten list of "Things I Need to Do", it seems rather pointless. You have to wonder who in the world is advising Mr. Zelaya.

GAUGING THE WILL OF THE PEOPLE

November 18, 2009

On March 23, 2009, President Manuel Zelaya issued Executive Decree No. PCM-05-2009 ordering that a fourth ballot box or *la cuarta urna* be placed at each of the polling stations throughout Honduras during the national elections on November 29. The boxes were to be positioned beside the three ballot boxes designated for casting votes for president, Congressional representatives, and local mayors. The purpose of the fourth ballot box would be to vote on a binding referendum on the question of whether or not to review the current Constitution of Honduras and rewrite it – supposedly so that it better represented the interests of the majority of the people in Honduras.

According to the decree, there was to be one question on the ballot, having to do with whether you were for or against reviewing and rewriting the Constitution. During the weeks that followed, President Zelaya proposed holding a non-binding opinion poll to gauge the mood of the public regarding the setting up of this fourth ballot box. He ultimately decided to hold the poll or *encuesta* on Sunday, June 28. On Saturday, June 27, the wording of the proposed poll was published in the government's official newspaper, *La Gaceta*. The wording, however, did not just mention setting up a fourth ballot box, but included a second question. That second question asked that if you favored a fourth ballot box, would you also favor the establishment of a National Constituent Assembly (*Constituyente*) to undertake the process of reviewing and rewriting the Constitution. *La Constituyente* would supposedly consist of a more diverse representation of Honduran society.

With the publication of the poll's text in *La Gaceta*, it became clear to members of the Legislative and Judicial branches of the Honduran government, as well as to Honduras' Attorney General and Armed Forces, that Mr. Zelaya was not simply moving to gauge the public's interest in a fourth ballot box on November 29, but in the same breath trying to gauge public support for *la Constituyente*.

The concern (fear, really) was that President Zelaya would manipulate the poll to his advantage (particularly given that the poll ballots had been printed in Venezuela) and not only succeed in setting up a fourth ballot box, but also win a vote for convening *la Constituyente* even before November 29. *La Constituyente* could then be used to help diffuse opposition to the fourth ballot box from Congress, the Supreme Court, and the Attorney General.

Mr. Zelaya is correct when he has argued on numerous occasions that the poll was meant to be non-binding. The problem, as seen by the institutions that supported his overthrow on Sunday, June 28, was that the poll, if successfully manipulated by President Zelaya, would have given him the incentive and the excuse for moving to establish *la Constituyente* as a counter-balance against all those who opposed him.

The critical point to remember here is that President Hugo Chávez of Venezuela and President Rafael Correa of Ecuador had already established a model in which they successfully set up *Constituyentes* and granted them full legislative powers, which the *Constituyentes* then utilized to dissolve both the Venezuelan Congress and Ecuadoran Congress.

If President Zelaya had been allowed to follow this Chávez-Correa model to its conclusion, then Honduras would by now probably have a *Constituyente* with full legislative powers, and it is possible that this new legislature would have already attempted (perhaps successfully) to dissolve the Honduran Congress. This would have made it very difficult to have blocked any creative maneuvers by President Zelaya to "work the system" to try and remain in power for an indefinite period of time... much the same way as Mr. Chávez has done and Mr. Correa is doing.

It is inaccurate to say that the political crisis in Honduras began on June 28. To be fair, you have to go back to at least March 23 when President Zelaya came out with his decree for *la cuarta urna*. How ironic that back then there was so much enthusiasm for the November 29 elections displayed by Mr. Zelaya's supporters. That fourth ballot box was seen as some sort of "silver bullet" that would initiate a process to change the Constitution and magically solve all of Honduras' problems of social and economic inequity and injustice. The upcoming elections no longer have the same appeal to those who were once so enthusiastic about letting the will of the people be heard.

CAUDILLOS NO FRIENDS OF THE POOR

November 24, 2009

Hopefully, whoever wins the upcoming presidential election in Honduras will have learned from the events of the past five months that the status quo in the country is not sustainable, and that he must not allow himself to be lulled into a "business as usual" attitude. After all that Honduras has been through and with three-quarters of Hondurans still living in poverty, complacency and apathy by the country's leaders should be a thing of the past. But neither should Honduras' new leader think of himself as a savior, because no one individual – no matter how well-intentioned or talented – can solve the country's problems. Rather than start off every sentence with "I", the new president of Honduras would be well-advised to adopt "We" as a staple of his speeches.

The danger with saviors in Latin America is that they often tend to become *caudillos*, authoritarian populists who justify everything they do in the name of helping the masses of people who are poor and powerless.

Unfortunately, *caudillos* usually end up not really being the friends of the poor and powerless that they appear to be. On the surface, *caudillos* make a lot of promises that are seldom fulfilled – there is almost never any follow-up, maintenance and repair, or fine-tuning. Mostly there's just a declaration of success or victory, regardless of the facts. The promises have the effect of creating high expectations and a tremendous amount of false hope, which leave people feeling more discouraged and disillusioned than before.

And when the people complain that a promise has not been kept, *caudillos* simply proceed to blame their failures on those within the evil elite class who seek to undermine everything, because *caudillos* do not see any advantage to accepting responsibility unless it benefits them. And of course *caudillos* are not encumbered by shame.

Caudillos mainly seek power for themselves. By dividing society and creating chaos, they confuse and weaken their opponents. They obtain the love and adulation of the people by pretending to be with them and of them, and by handing out money and other trinkets and prizes to them.

Instead of empowering people, *caudillos* make people weaker by making them more dependent on their goodwill and benevolence... much in the same way as lords treated peasants during medieval times. *Caudillos* have no ideology, no philosophy of life, no vision... just one guiding principle, one true loyalty, and that is to themselves. They are vain like peacocks, and love themselves to a degree that many of us would consider silly or even unhealthy.

NOTES

All the world is a stage for Manuel Zelaya, and so he views everything around him as props to enhance his celebrity. The idea of quietly leading without much fanfare, self-adulation, or self-promotion is an alien concept to a *caudillo* such as Mr. Zelaya. The thought of not taking credit for something is unthinkable, nonsensical, and even repulsive to demagogues.

⚜

MEL'S SMOKING MIRRORS

November 24, 2009

Mr. Zelaya loves to take credit for the relatively high growth rates of Honduras' economy during 2005-2008. If you only look at the figures that he gives, it would be tempting to think, "Hmm, not bad". Be careful, though, because simple figures do not always provide the full extent of the story. Numbers can be manipulated to tell whatever narrative you like. Governments routinely do this to support their records.

In the case of economic growth in Honduras, it is important to understand the primary sources of revenue in the country. By far, the biggest generator of revenue are remittances from Hondurans living and working abroad, primarily in the United States. The closest other revenue generating industries are *maquilas* and tourism, and each of them comes in at well under $1 billion per year.

Honduras' Central Bank has been tracking remittances for many years. In 2001, remittances to Honduras were estimated at $460 million; in 2002, $770 million; in 2003, $862 million; in 2004, $1.134 billion; in 2005, $1.763 billion; in 2006; $2.359 billion; in 2007, approximately $3 billion; and in 2008, $2.7 billion.

Note the significantly higher levels of remittances during 2006-2008. Those were the first three years of the Zelaya administration, when Hondurans continued to feel so desperate about the economic and security conditions in their country that they opted to emigrate to the US. The more Hondurans emigrated, the greater the flow of money sent back to families in Honduras, and voilà... more economic growth.

Mr. Zelaya is claiming credit for the growth of Honduras' economy when in fact he should be ashamed that the main reason the economy grew was due to remittances. A country that relies on remittances from its nationals abroad is a poorly governed country. Not only is Mr. Zelaya not ashamed, he twists the facts in order to polish his record and benefit himself. He is deliberately deceptive, and this deception is sadly targeted at his loyal followers, feeding them false information and thus false hope. Those who know better are not fooled by Mr. Zelaya's stastistics.

Another achievement Mr. Zelaya loves to reference is that during the first two years of his administration, poverty was reduced by ten percent. That must be some sort of record for a developing country. Ten percent in 24 months? That is truly amazing. How in the world could anyone possibly be against a leader who has brought so much development and progress to Honduras in such a short time? This was a bogus claim by Mr. Zelaya. A ten percent reduction in poverty would have been noticeably felt in Honduras and would have won Mr. Zelaya international recognition as a genius in the field of development economics. Neither occurred.

NOTES

Before Mr. Zelaya came to office, President Maduro and Cardinal Rodríguez traveled the world begging to have Honduras' foreign debt pardoned. They promised that Honduras had learned its lessons and would make sure that in the future it would not borrow irresponsibly. As part of the World Bank's program for Highly Indebted Poor Countries

(HIPC), most if not all of Honduras' foreign debt was pardoned. Mel started with almost a clean slate, so he was at liberty to start spending to his heart's content. Since Honduras had relatively little debt after Mr. Maduro's administration, banks were more than glad to start lending to Honduras again, which allowed Mr. Zelaya to spend freely on social programs and fuel yet another cycle of unsustainable foreign indebtedness by the country.

Fear of Autocracies

November 25, 2009

Fear is a powerful, though unhealthy and unpredictable, motivator. When the history of the current political crisis in Honduras is written it will show that Mr. Zelaya's growing relationship with and near idol worship of Hugo Chávez was the primary reason for his ousting. Yes, there was that whole *cuarta urna* thing and talk of setting up a National Constituent Assembly to rewrite the Constitution. Yes, there was the sudden 60 percent spike in the minimum wage. And yes, there was Mel's annoying habit of inciting the mobs and ignoring the other branches of government and his own party. But it was really the rising presence and influence of Mr. Chávez and his ALBA colleagues in the affairs of Honduras that began to spook everyone.

For better or worse, Mr. Chávez instills fear in many Hondurans because of what they see happening in Venezuela. Venezuela has become an autocracy ruled by a "strongman" who bullies, belittles and trounces anyone who dares to oppose him. Although at their core, autocrats like Mr. Chávez are infantile and paranoid, on the surface they appear to be invincible, and it is this concentration of so much power that is traditionally feared because it is hard get rid of autocrats once they become entrenched.

Hondurans tend to be able to resign themselves to poor, or even corrupt, political leaders. What they do not seem to want to tolerate are poor and corrupt leaders who wish to remain in power indefinitely and change the balance of power in the country too quickly and too much in their own favor. You cannot do too much good in four short years as president. On the other hand, you cannot do but so much bad, and that's kind of the *modus operandi* under which the majority of Hondurans appear willing to exist.

NOTES

1. Mr. Zelaya is a victim of a much broader agenda. *"Comandante Vaquero"*, as Mr. Chávez affectionately dubbed him, is merely an actor in a play written, directed, produced and marketed by Mr. Chávez. Defending Honduran democracy is only a pretense. Mr. Chávez is primarily concerned with expanding his power and influence in Latin America and the Caribbean. He sees Honduras as a battleground.

2. Under the close tutelage of Mr. Chávez, Mel would have led Honduras into an abyss. With all of its oil and natural gas, Venezuela should be a well-off nation, but instead it suffers most of the same problems that plague poor, developing countries. The fact is that Mr. Chávez's so-called "21st Century Socialism" is not all it's cracked up to be. Imagine what Mr. Chávez's model of development would have done to Honduras – a country with only a fraction of Venezuela's economic advantages.

Putting Aside Tribalism

November 25, 2009

It is amazing to see rallies for democracy and peace of 50,000 to 100,000 people in San Pedro Sula and Tegucigalpa, and witness such a high spirit of unity in Honduras – not so much against Mr. Zelaya but against what he represented through his relationships with Mr. Chávez and ALBA. Seeing this raises the question of whether Hondurans could come together, at least for the next four years, under a kind of "Unity Coalition", rather than going back to the old party politics of Liberal and Nationalist, Red and Blue, and all the other colors. Anything seems possible right now.

If Honduras is ever going to make some progress in developing into a stable and just society, Hondurans have to relinquish their "tribalism" – pride and loyalty to partisan traditions, philosophies, melodies, colors, flags, and mascots. Mr. Zelaya has been entirely correct in identifying the fact that the status quo in Honduras is unjust and unsustainable. The gap in income inequality is too great. Mel's methods and philosophy for changing the status quo were divisive, destructive and uninspired, but he was right about the central problem in Honduras... social injustice.

Mel Zelaya is not the devil, he's just a regular guy with too much ego for his own good. He surrounded himself with poor advisers. He got lost, went astray. But, initially at least, he had some good intentions. Now it's time to take advantage of an opening that Mr. Zelaya has handed Honduras. There is a window of opportunity for Hondurans to begin to use their new-found sense of unity for the betterment of all Hondurans, especially the approximately 75 percent of the population that remains relatively powerless and without a voice – a disenfranchised majority.

A unity coalition government is not that outrageous. The Nationalist Party and the Liberal Party, along with the Christian Democracy Party, the Democratic Unification Party, and the Innovation and Unity Party, could simply agree to govern together by sharing key cabinet positions. There's your real "Government of Unity and National Reconciliation". Because let's face it, the one pushed under the Tegucigalpa-San José Accord was a flop.

It would be a huge step for whoever wins the presidency this Sunday to surround himself on a daily basis with leaders of the other parties and find ways to govern rather than just rule, and develop a 20-year vision for Honduras jointly, through creative consensus... as Hondurans, not as tribes. What an innovation, and what a message to the international community.

NOTES

1. Euphoria is evident in the massive peace and democracy rallies in Tegucigalpa, San Pedro Sula, La Ceiba, Choluteca, Danli, El Progreso and other cities and towns in Honduras – tens of thousands of people wearing white, rather than the traditional major party colors of blue or red. Once people come down from their highs, the challenge will be to be kind and gracious, not just to those who shared the good feelings... but especially to the many who did not.

2. Honduras has an opportunity to show the world that it is capable of thinking creatively and multi-dimensionally, and not get stuck bickering about right and wrong. Honduras must aggressively take the lead in trying to come up with proposals for reconciliation. The OAS has become too politicized and influenced by Mr. Chávez and his cheerleaders. Mr. Zelaya must be brought back into the fold (not as president but as participant) by showing him some respect and reassuring him that he will not be imprisoned. He will have to demonstrate a good faith effort to participate in a process of reconciliation that excludes any foreign involvement or influence.

✠

Only Good Guys are Worthy

November 28, 2009

Many Hondurans feel that engaging in an electoral process to choose the future political leaders of the country in the midst of ongoing uncertainty and disagreement over the status of a democratically elected president who was forcefully deposed is not right. But it is disingenuous for those who oppose the elections to rationalize their position by proudly arguing, "Look at all the countries around the world that will not recognize the elections", and then when a country has a change of heart and opts to recognize the elections, they respond, "Ah well, that country doesn't really count or matter". So long as a country supports their position, it is deemed legitimate – the "good guy". However, if that country happens to change its position, then suddenly it is no longer legitimate – and it is a "bad guy".

At one point, it did not look as if the United States would recognize the elections. Those who oppose the elections found it convenient to paint the US as a good guy and totally worthy. Now, things look a little different. The US will recognize the elections, and so it is no longer worthy. A week ago, the argument went like this... "Well yes, but what would you expect of the US, they've never been trustworthy, and besides it's only one country; everybody else is against the elections". Then came Panama. "Okay, well... it's only the US and Panama." Then came Canada and Colombia. "Well, of course they have to obey the US." Then there's Mexico. Don't expect it to side with Mr. Zelaya after he insulted President Calderón. The rationalizations have continued even with Perú's decision to support the elections. The latest addition is Costa Rica.

In the meantime, other major democratic countries like Germany and Japan, and smaller ones like Israel, South Korea and Taiwan have expressed their support for the elections. Italy is leaning strongly in favor. The United Kingdom will probably support them too. There is division on this issue within the Western Hemisphere and in Europe. A long list of Latin American nations, led by Brazil and Venezuela, will not recognize the elections. Spain has consistently and strongly come out against the elections. France is probably in this camp as well.

The existence of a growing divide within the international community should prompt some reflection among those who oppose the elections tomorrow. At the very least, it should prompt a re-evaluation of the now rather stale argument that because the entire world sees the election as invalid, ergo they must be invalid.

NOTES

In today's edition of *El Heraldo*, there is an article that quotes César Ham (one of Mel Zelaya's closest supporters) of the Democratic Unification (UD) Party as saying that Mr. Zelaya admitted to him that he won his election through fraud. The temptation is to jump on this and hold it up as a clear admission of corruption on the part of Mr. Zelaya. But Mr. Zelaya's comments should be placed in the proper context. What Mr. Zelaya means is that electoral fraud is a systemic problem in the country, and thus that his campaigns and those of his opponents have likely been guilty of fraud. This does not excuse the fraud, but merely suggests that Mr. Zelaya is not admitting to intentionally committing fraud. Not sure there is much of a news story here... only a sad commentary on yet another flaw in the Honduran system of government.

ANOTHER RANCHER FROM OLANCHO

November 30, 2009

There may be no one in the world who understands deposed president Manuel Zelaya better than the newly-elected president, Porfirio Lobo. They share an awful lot in common. For starters, each is rather charismatic and informal in his own way. Mr. Zelaya prefers to be called "Mel", which is short for Manuel. Mr. Lobo goes by "Pepe", short for Porfirio. Both men hail from the department of Olancho, which is Honduras' version of the old Wild West. Blood feuds abound in Olancho, so it's common knowledge in Honduras that it's not a good idea to cross an *Olanchano*. Both are former ranchers and have been involved in the forestry business. Likewise, both men are from the wealthy class and had fathers who wielded significant power in Olanchan political circles.

Pepe and Mel belong more or less to the same generation. Pepe is 61 years old, and Mel is 57. Pepe first became involved in party politics as a teenager. For much of his early adult life, he was an active member of the Nationalist Party. He was elected to the Honduran Congress in 1990. He served as the president of the Congress from 2002 to 2006. Mel joined the Liberal Party in 1970 and was an active politician from the mid-1980s through most of the 1990s as a member of Congress. In 2005, Pepe and Mel ran against each other for the presidency. Mel won by a very close margin. So both men are politically savvy and understand the language and ways of government in Honduras.

Perhaps the most interesting thing about Pepe and Mel is that they understand each other's political thinking. Although Pepe is a Nationalist, and thus conservative, and Mel is a Liberal, each one has toyed with opposite political philosophies. During the 1980s, Pepe studied in then-communist Moscow, which created at least a perception that he was leftist-leaning. Mel, on the other hand, has long been known as a conservative Liberal. It's only been in the past year and a half that Mel, through his growing association with Hugo Chávez of Venezuela, has shifted to the far left. Pepe and Mel understand each other's views, even if they do not agree with them.

What all this means is that the election of Pepe Lobo, more than anything, could help Honduras with the still unresolved dilemma of what to do about Mr. Zelaya. After all, Mr. Zelaya remains in the Brazilian embassy in Tegucigalpa, and he is now weighing the possibility of seeking political asylum in neighboring Nicaragua, where he could continue to pose problems for Honduras (or at least be extremely annoying) for the foreseeable future. It would be ironic indeed if the one person who succeeds in soothing Mel's bruised ego and finding a way to make a deal with Mr. Zelaya that allows Honduran society to begin patching up its divisions and finding ways to work together is Mr. Zelaya's old political nemesis and fellow Olanchan.

PUTTING AN END TO THE MEL-O-DRAMA

December 2, 2009

It is unlikely that Honduras' Congress today will vote in favor of reinstating Manuel Zelaya as president. Mr. Zelaya may win between 25 to 35 of the 128 votes that will be cast, but he needs 65. At least 20 of the Liberal Party members of Congress have publicly announced their support for reinstating Mr. Zelaya, including Carolina Echeverría, Javier Hall Polío, Eleazar Juárez, Erick Rodríguez, Elvia Argentina Valle, and Margarita Zelaya. Congresswoman Marleny Paz of the Christian Democracy (DC) Party will vote for reinstatement. All five members of the Democratic Unification (UD) Party will likely back Mr. Zelaya. These include Silvia Ayala, Doris Gutierrez, César Ham, Óscar Mejia, and Marvin Ponce. So what happens next?

There are numerous possible scenarios, including one that has Mr. Zelaya leaving the Brazilian embassy of his own accord and agreeing to stand trial for a list of alleged crimes, including abuse of power, treason, and corruption. The trial could drag on for weeks or months. But this would be a depressing distraction for Honduran society and a problem for the new president, Pepe Lobo, who appears more interested in looking to the future and trying to find ways to begin to heal the divisions in Honduras and get to work on the vast array of neglected issues facing the country – much in the same way President Obama chose to put aside allegations of misconduct during the Bush administration and move forward. A trial would keep Mr. Zelaya in the limelight, which is what he always enjoys and thrives on. It would add fuel to the Resistance movement, which would take advantage of a trial to try to complete the transformation of Mr. Zelaya into a martyr to help get traction for its cause of a National Constituent Assembly.

Another scenario has Mr. Zelaya being given political asylum in another country such as Brazil or Nicaragua. But Mr. Zelaya doesn't speak Portuguese, and Brazil seems a world away, both geographically and culturally. Nicaragua would be right next door to Honduras, which would be convenient if Mr. Zelaya wished to continue being an annoyance. But Mr. Zelaya isn't all that popular in Nicaragua after the ruckus he caused back in late-July and early-August in the Nicaraguan town of Ocotal trying to organize a border insurrection. Besides, Nicaragua is poorer even than Honduras, and not much fun, particularly with Daniel Ortega stirring up trouble again with his efforts to manipulate the Nicaraguan Constitution and get re-elected. Sound familiar?

Mexico would be great... not too far away and lots of fun things to do. José Miguel Insulza spent much of the 1980s in Mexico as a political exile from the Pinochet regime. In fact, that's where he met his wife, Georgina. But Mr. Zelaya burned his bridges with President Calderón during his visit to Mexico City in early-July by trying to be clever and curry favor with opposition leader Andrés López Obrador. So Mexico is out. It is doubtful that Mr. Chávez will take Mel. He has enough problems in Venezuela at the moment, and he's probably not too happy with Mr. Zelaya, given the millions of petro dollars he invested in his Honduran experiment with so little to show for it. Besides, Mr. Zelaya really would not be comfortable anywhere except Honduras. He does not have that natural curiosity for or ease of adapting to foreign lands. He shares that trait with George W. Bush. Remember how awkward, uncomfortable and in-a-hurry-to-get-home President Bush looked every time he traveled abroad?

There is always the option of keeping things as they are. Mr. Zelaya could remain sequestered in the Brazilian embassy throughout the Christmas holidays and into the New Year. He sits back and watches Mr. Lobo's inauguration on television, and continues the drama into 2010. Brazil's president, Luiz Lula, has said that Mel is welcome to stay at the embassy as long as he wants. For that matter, so has President Micheletti. But this is not such a great scenario either because it doesn't solve anything. Mr. Zelaya would just continue to suck wind from the next administration. The drama would go on day after day. Mr. Zelaya is nothing if not cheerfully stubborn.

There are an awful lot of people in Honduras saying, "Just put the guy away and toss the key, for gosh sake!... forget the trial." But that's not going to happen because it does not do anything to encourage reconciliation in the country, as Mr. Lobo wants and Honduras needs. If anything, it would exacerbate the bad feelings that many Hondurans already have for each other because of the events of the past year. Mr. Zelaya has a significant following in Honduras, although it is not as sizable or passionate as his supporters would like to think. But it may well be larger and better organized than those who oppose him dare to imagine.

Assuming that Congress will not vote to reinstate Mr. Zelaya tomorrow, where does that leave the country? President Lula may have given a small clue yesterday all the way from Estoril, Portugal. Trying to brainstorm ways in which there could be a meeting of minds with Mr. Lobo on normalizing relations between Brazil and Honduras, Mr. Lula offered the idea that Mr. Zelaya be formally reinstated for at least the ceremonial transfer of presidential powers to Mr. Lobo on January 27, 2010. In other words, that Mr. Zelaya and not Mr. Micheletti preside over the honors that day. This would provide political symbolism that allows everyone to save face and prove that no one backed down from their principles. Not too long ago, powerful Honduran businessman and Zelaya opponent, Adolfo Facusse, proposed something similar... a short symbolic reinstatement of a day or even a few hours.

The plan sounds ludicrous, and it would force a lot of people to swallow some humble pie. With so many people wanting vengeance for all the havoc that Mr. Zelaya has wreaked on Honduras, it would all feel like a slap in the face. But hold on. Remember that there are also a lot of people out there wanting payback for what they perceive as the trauma of an unjustifiable and unforgivable "coup d'état". Mr. Lobo is all too aware of the Herculean task ahead of him. He is a seasoned politician who knows the Honduran people. The "Two Americas" that US Senator John Edwards talked about and coined in his presidential campaign stump speeches is nothing compared to the divisions in Honduran society right now, and what they could become in the future if Mr. Lobo miscalculates.

It is possible that, over the next seven weeks, a deal may be arranged to bring Mr. Zelaya back into the fold in a limited but visible capacity. It would not be a complete surprise to see Mr. Zelaya attend Mr. Lobo's swearing-in ceremony, or even see him given a ceremonial role as a symbolic gesture of respect in the interest of national reconciliation.

NOTES

Mr. Zelaya is now apparently rejecting the Micheletti government's letter of safe-passage to Mexico because he does not recognize the legitimacy of the interim government. He is asking the Mexican government to receive him not as a political asylee but rather as an "honored guest". This change of heart resulted in the Mexican aircraft sent to Tegucigalpa by President Calderón to pick up Mel to be redirected to San Pedro Sula, pending negotiations about his status.

DIFFERENTIATING MEL AND CAUSE

December 3, 2009

Following Wednesday evening's overwhelming 111-14 vote by Congress to reject the reinstatement of Manuel Zelaya as president, Roberto Micheletti proclaimed, "Mel is now history". While Mr. Micheletti may not be far off the mark, it would be ill-advised to assume that just because Mr. Zelaya has squandered his fifteen minutes of fame that the cause which he represented will now also be put to rest. Nothing could be further from the truth.

Regardless of the way one feels about Mr. Zelaya, he provided a sense of hope for about one-third of the Honduran population. It was a false hope, but it was hope nonetheless. Mel's supporters hoped that he would help change an inequitable and unjust social and economic status quo in Honduras where three-quarters of the population lives on three dollars or less daily, and half of that segment lives on one dollar or less per day.

Almost everyone in Honduras acknowledges that the cause toward which the hope has been aimed is a good one. Very few Hondurans believe that having so much imbalance and poverty in the country is a good thing, either from a moral standpoint or from the more selfish standpoint of security and stability. With so many people in Honduras simply struggling to survive and feed their families, there is no way anyone in Honduran society can ever feel safe and at peace. The disagreement has never been whether or not the status quo must be changed, but how and when.

Mr. Zelaya lacked the leadership abilities, emotional strength, and creative talent needed to define a unique vision for a better Honduras. He was incapable of leading through inspiration rather the coercion. In the end, he lost the trust of a huge portion of the population and, by pitting classes against each other, he succeeded admirably in polarizing Honduran society... so much so that friendships, acquaintances and family relationships were destroyed, perhaps irrevocably. Within a society that was already filled with fear, Mr. Zelaya injected more fear. Whatever crimes Mr. Zelaya has allegedly committed, none can be worse than consciously and deliberately moving to turn Hondurans against each other.

So yes, Mel is probably history. But the cause still exists. All you have to do is look at the thousands of Hondurans who have consistently been marching in the streets and demonstrating in the parks. Yes, they have been calling for the reinstatement of Mr. Zelaya. But that is their "position", not the essence of what they want and need. What they want is to have a more representative voice in the way Honduras is governed. What they want is more of a balance of power vis-a-vis those "elites" that Mr. Zelaya cynically blames for all the problems that exist in the country. That is why the Resistance movement in Honduras wants to establish a National Constituent Assembly that will then undertake a process of rewriting the Constitution to re-invent the country's system of government. The assumption is that that is the only viable solution.

The political crisis in Honduras has always been too narrowly defined. For the past year, the debate has been about whether or not to set up *la cuarta urna*, whether the ousting of Mr. Zelaya was a coup or not a coup, whether it was legal or illegal, who is a *golpista* and who is a true lover of democracy, who is lying and who is telling the truth, or whether Mel is a criminal or a hero. All of these are dead end debates. The real question has to do with how we transform Honduras into a truly representative democracy that gives relatively equal weight to the interests of the vast majority of the Honduran people who continue to have little or no voice. One way certainly could be the *la Constituyente*, but it is not the only strategy that could be on the table.

NOTES

1. One of the reasons that Manuel Zelaya did such a poor job as president is that he did not spend enough time at home doing the grunt work to solve the problems of Honduras. He made grand promises and may indeed have had the best interests of the poor in mind, but his attention span is limited and he seems to get quickly bored with the minutiae involved in effectively addressing complex issues. His true passion is making speeches and riding in parades. At heart, he is a showman.

2. Changing the status quo in Honduras should not focus on forcibly redistributing wealth. It does no good to alienate the business class because it is Honduras' business community that provides the bulk of the jobs in the country. Changing the status quo starts with great and visionary leadership which focuses on inspiring both the business community and average citizens to willingly and enthusiastically invest a greater portion of their human and financial capital in the empowerment of the people of Honduras, primarily the poor and powerless. Great leaders inspire and unite rather than coerce and divide. Mr. Zelaya coerced and divided.

CAUDILLOS MAKE POOR
ADVOCATES OF THE PEOPLE

December 5, 2009

The decision by Juan Barahona and the National Resistance Front to give up trying to push for the reinstatement of Manuel Zelaya as president reflects an acceptance of hard reality. For better or worse, Mr. Zelaya will not return to power, and so the Resistance will have to look for another way to achieve its aim of establishing a National Constituent Assembly. Now, with the removal of Mr. Zelaya as the primary issue, there may be some room for a healthy and reasoned discussion between the leaders of the Resistance and the government of Porfirio Lobo. Mr. Zelaya has taken up an awful lot of space, and most of it has been dedicated to recovering what he personally lost rather than advocating for the people who have been marching and demonstrating in the streets on his behalf.

While you can argue that what is at the center of Mr. Zelaya's agenda is the cause of justice and equality for the poor and relatively powerless in Honduras, the vast portion of Mr. Zelaya's rhetoric since he was ousted on June 28 has been about him. It has been about recovering his presidency at any cost, including a willingness to compromise on the single most important item on the Resistance movement's agenda – *la Constituyente.* Occasionally, Mr. Zelaya has peppered his rambling speeches and interviews with the idea that all he wants is to restore democracy to Honduras, but you always end up with a sense that democracy to Mr. Zelaya simply means a nation in which he leads and everyone else follows faithfully and blindly, trusting that he knows best.

Mr. Zelaya has a habit of referring to himself as the "servant" of the people... *tu servidor.* Yet clearly he is more comfortable having people serve him. He has a habit also of demonizing the wealthy class of Honduras. He does these things so often that it is possible to be lulled into believing that this is a true man of the people, someone who really understands their plight because he has lived and worked with them side by side, someone whose strength and vision emanate from a deep selflessness and humility. But this has not been the Mel Zelaya the world has seen and heard. Quite the opposite.

In both tone and content, Mr. Zelaya has consistently displayed his *caudillo* heritage... someone who wants to lead the people and be loved by the people, but who will never be fully with the people because he has never been of the people. To him and many of his close advisers who belong to the same elite class, the agenda of the poor and relatively powerless is more of an intellectual exercise than something they truly understand. What Mr. Zelaya has is more akin to sympathy than empathy.

Mr. Zelaya and many of his advisers have led privileged lives. They are politicians and business people who socialize with other politicians and business people. They would make good advocates if you wanted to make something happen within the existing system of power and privilege, but they are poor advocates if you want to radically change the existing system.

So I wish Mr. Barahona and others like Rafael Alegría, Father Andrés Tamayo and Berta Cáceres Flores well in their cause. They have a long struggle ahead, but at least now they can focus and develop a pragmatic strategy to gain what they want, rather than trying to piggyback on a *caudillo's* personal crusade.

NOTES

Manuel Zelaya is only a small part of the problem in Honduras. However, it is important to try to paint as accurate a picture of Mr. Zelaya as possible so that we understand that the image of this man that many would like to market is a false one. Note that criticism of Mr. Zelaya does not necessarily imply approval of the manner in which he was removed from power.

THE INSANITY OF MANIPULATED REPRESENTATION

December 11, 2009

Just how would the National Resistance Front's proposed National Constituent Assembly be elected, function, and be re-elected? The idea of a legislative body that would better represent the interests of all Hondurans is a noble one. However, most of what we have heard about *la Constituyente* are slogans and almost nothing in the way of a concrete, well-crafted plan for how it would all work. If such a document exists, I would love to review it.

La Constituyente seems to be a romantic notion that a legislature that is more beholden to the interests of laborers, peasant workers, indigenous tribes, and the poor in general would be less corrupt, less apt to be manipulated, wiser, and a better promoter of the public good than any Congress. On what assumptions is this notion based?

Given the close and growing relationship between the administration of President Zelaya and the government of President Hugo Chávez of Venezuela prior to Mr. Zelaya's ousting, it is reasonable to assume *la Constituyente* in Honduras may eventually have come to resemble the National Assembly of Venezuela, which is a unicameral body made up of 167 representatives. These "deputies" (*diputados*) are elected by "universal, direct, personal, and secret" vote on a national party-list proportional representation system.

The "universal and "direct" parts are obvious and straightforward, but "personal" and "secret" are less clear, and open the door for all sorts of non-democratic practices. The proportional representation seems okay, particularly given that most of the world's democracies use this system rather than one based on the "winner-take-all" system used in the United States. Elections where a candidate only has to win a plurality of the votes in order to be elected to represent a particular district has the unfair effect of leaving significant blocs of voters unrepresented.

There is nothing inherently wrong with a proportional representation-based National Constituent Assembly. But could it work in Honduras? Venezuela's *Asamblea Nacional* includes three seats that are reserved for representatives of the country's indigenous tribes. Seems fair enough, given that they were the original inhabitants of the land.

The more critical question is, "Could a National Constituent Assembly remain any more independent and less swayed by private interests than the Congress?" We know that Congress has a strong lean in favor of the economic and social interests of the wealthy business class in Honduras. It's not right and it's not fair because it leaves the vast majority of Hondurans at a significant disadvantage. To whom would representatives of a National Constituent Assembly established under the Zelaya administration have answered? To their constituencies? Maybe. Maybe not.

If you look at the recent history of Venezuela's *Asamblea Nacional*, notice that in 2000 it granted Mr. Chávez temporary power to rule by decree. Rule by decree? Sounds a little too much like a dictatorship. Mr. Chávez approved 49 laws by decree. Then, in January 2007, the *Asamblea Nacional* granted Mr. Chávez another 18 months to rule by decree and push through a series of revolutionary economic and social laws that transformed Venezuela into a socialist society.

Venezuela's *Asamblea Nacional* placed its faith and trust in one guy. One guy. That is about the farthest thing from a democracy imaginable. What if that one guy just happens to get up on the wrong side of the bed one morning? What if he's got some bad habits that cloud his judgment? What if he's got too much of an ego for his own good? What if he's got prejudices toward certain races, ethnic groups or religious faiths? What if he suddenly gets the urge to nationalize everything in town? What if he simply wants to stick around forever?

One of the defining elements of a democracy is a system of checks and balances. In countries like Honduras, this system unfortunately is manipulated by the segment of the society that is wealthy and privileged. This has to change. But to trade this kind of system in for one that can potentially be manipulated by a single person is, well... insanity.

NOTES

Does the idea of establishing a National Constituent Assembly in Honduras to review and rewrite the Constitution have any merit at all? Would the idea be more plausible had it not been pushed by Mr. Zelaya but rather by someone who was not such a polarizing figure and commanded the respect, trust, and confidence of Honduran society as a whole? Clearly, there is a need in Honduras to change the social and economic status quo. Either it will change peacefully or it may change violently. Is the best way to do this through a National Constituent Assembly that includes a much more diverse representation of the Honduran people? The assumption is that such a body would not replace the Congress but rather only be formed temporarily to review and rewrite the Constitution. Is this assumption reasonable? Would representatives of a National

Constituent Assembly willingly relinquish power and return to their previous jobs? Or would they succumb to the temptation to make the Assembly permanent in order to create a balance of power with the Congress? Even more, would there be too much of a temptation to simply dissolve the Congress and replace it with the Assembly? The central question is, "Does the Constitution need to be rewritten in order to allow for a more just society?"

GREAT LEADERS DO NOT FEAR PRISON

December 15, 2009

Between the time Manuel Zelaya was arrested and exiled from Honduras on June 28 and the day he began his self-imprisonment in the Brazilian embassy on September 21, Manuel Zelaya flew up and down the Western Hemisphere aboard a luxury business jet graciously provided by his friend Hugo Chávez of Venezuela. Mr. Zelaya traveled with an entourage, stayed at expensive hotels, ate well, shopped, and gave lots of speeches. He was greeted with honors and given the red carpet treatment by several heads of state and was photographed countless times smiling and shaking hands with people of power and influence... you know, the elite.

During the past eleven weeks, Mr. Zelaya has remained safe, if not entirely comfortable, in Brazil's diplomatic mission in Tegucigalpa, trying to keep international attention focused on him by constantly giving interviews, writing letters on his leftover stash of official presidential stationary, and forever making calls on his cell phone to world leaders asking them not to forget his plight.

Throughout this time, supporters of Mr. Zelaya have marched daily in the streets of Honduran cities and towns beneath the hot sun. Even Mr. Zelaya's wife, Xiomara, was initially out there on the ground among the people. Thousands of good people have placed their trust in Mr. Zelaya and have faithfully awaited his climactic return – much in the same way as the early Christians in the first century awaited the second coming of Jesus Christ. Until the Honduran Congress overwhelmingly voted against reinstating Mr. Zelaya on December 2, thousands of people continued to hope that Mr. Zelaya would somehow pull a rabbit out of his hat and regain the office from which he was ingloriously removed.

Now, after the election of Porfirio Lobo to be Honduras' next president, it is finally beginning to dawn on Mr. Zelaya's fans that the odyssey is coming to its anti-climactic conclusion. The struggle for the National Constituent Assembly may remain alive, but Mr. Zelaya will not recover his lost presidency. Even the most committed die-hards understand this at some level.

What is puzzling is the fact that, in the midst of Mr. Zelaya's repeated promises or threats to return to his homeland prior to September 21, there was never anything actually preventing him from purchasing an airline ticket, boarding a commercial aircraft, and flying to Tegucigalpa. The problem was that Mr. Zelaya did not wish to be arrested again and, this time, imprisoned and brought up to face a series of political and criminal charges before the Supreme Court of Justice. Thus, he opted to sneak back into Honduras – much like the Greeks entered Troy – and then proceeded to at times unilaterally declare victory and other times play the persecuted injured soul. It is as if he cannot seem to decide which role plays better with his fascinated audience. Is it better to be admired for his audacity and courage, or does it make more sense to draw on peoples' sympathies?

It would be easier to respect and even admire a leader who willingly and bravely allowed himself to be imprisoned by the authorities he so loathes to make his point, rather than insist on remaining holed up in an embassy and making a lot of noise so that he will not fade completely from the headlines. His latest folly with the amateurish aid of the Mexican government to gain safe-passage out of Honduras is merely another example.

It is not clear beyond a shadow of a doubt that Mr. Zelaya committed any crimes worthy of his ousting. If anything, the one thing that seems rather certain is that Mr. Zelaya has a valid case to make that he was taken out of the country illegally. This sort of thing can't even be done to average citizens. So you have to wonder, "Why doesn't Mr. Zelaya boldly stand up for his rights?" His followers would certainly support him, and perhaps he would attain even greater celebrity status than the one he now cherishes.

Martin Luther King Jr. once said, "An individual who breaks a law that conscience tells him is unjust, and who willingly accepts the penalty of imprisonment in order to arouse the conscience of the community over its injustice, is in reality expressing the highest respect for the law." Many great leaders have willingly gone to prison (for years, in some cases) to stand up for their beliefs. Martin Luther King did. So did Nelson Mandela... Dietrich Bonhoeffer... Ghandi... Jesus of Nazareth. There are countless others throughout history. Mr. Zelaya has chosen a different path.

NOTES

Why has Mr. Zelaya not allowed himself to be imprisoned? Imprisonment would make him somewhat of a minor martyr, and it could add more fuel to the Resistance demonstrating for him. Mel may still be traumatized by all that has happened. It is more comfortable and ego-lifting shuttling up and down the hemisphere in a luxury jet with an entourage of advisers, and being greeted with full honors by heads of state. Being imprisoned implies a degree of uncertainty, discomfort, and lack of control that is scary. To truly great and serious leaders like King, Gandhi, and Mandela imprisonment is something that they welcomed because it allowed them to hold firm to their principles, make a point, and keep their causes alive. Imprisonment also allowed them some quiet time to reflect and write. Imprisonment holds no such appeal to average guys like Mel.

Those Evil Golpistas

December 15, 2009

So much of the conversation in Honduras that revolves around the overthrow of Manuel Zelaya as president has focused on whether one is a *golpista* (code for fascist) or not a *golpista* (code for "true believer in democracy"). The conversation goes absolutely nowhere useful, and those who persist in this labeling game do so because they are either lazy or lack the ability or desire to craft a thoughtful argument.

There are many people who support Manuel Zelaya and do not play this game, instead preferring to focus on Mel's efforts to help the poor and powerless in Honduras. They emphasize the fact that Mr. Zelaya was a democratically elected president who was removed from office at gunpoint and without so much as even a trial and an opportunity to defend himself. These individuals have a valid gripe.

The labeling game might make sense if those who engaged in it honestly believed that it is never right or permissible to use force to influence or change a situation. Very few people fall into this camp, especially individuals such as presidents Hugo Chávez or Daniel Ortega, who regularly speak fondly and nostalgically about revolutions.

You can argue that using force to remove a leader when that person is perceived to pose a threat is wrong based on the fallacy of the perception. But arguing that one who supports the use of force is automatically anti-democratic is overly narrow and illogical. There are few, if any, democratic nations or institutions that have not used force at one time or another.

President Obama has just approved a plan to deploy 30,000 more US troops to Afghanistan to fight against the Taliban and al-Qaeda. Ironically, yesterday he accepted the Nobel Peace Prize. In his acceptance speech, Mr. Obama refused to renounce war as a tool of foreign policy. He said, "A nonviolent movement could not have halted Hitler's armies. Negotiations cannot convince al-Qaida's leaders to lay down their arms. To say that force is sometimes necessary is not a call to cynicism, it is a recognition of history."

So how does the new US buildup in Afghanistan differ significantly from forcing Mr. Zelaya out of office? It doesn't really. Both moves were driven by self-interest and a fear of compromising national security. You can argue that both moves are illegal, unwise, lacking in imagination, or morally wrong.

But painting the originators of these plans (or those who support them) as fascists, terrorists, or simply bad people is hypocritical, unless you see the use of force as inherently evil and thus would willingly sacrifice your own well-being, and that of those you love, rather than use violence yourself. In such a case, the label *golpista* could be applied to almost anyone because very few people would be so morally pure.

⚜

PEPE'S GRAND NATIONAL DIALOGUE

December 16, 2009

The last "Grand National Dialogue" that took place in Honduras occurred under the administration of President Ricardo Maduro (2002-2006). By most estimates, that process was a failure because it did not succeed in developing a consensus on the social and economic priorities in the country and, more importantly, a long-term strategy for achieving them.

The first problem is that it did not continue. It disappeared from the headlines long before the end of Mr. Maduro's term in office. The process was short-lived, when it should have been designed to continue for as long as there exist divisions and massive poverty and inequities in Honduras.

The second problem with Mr. Maduro's *Gran Diálogo Nacional* is that it was structured in a way that allowed the traditional power players in Honduran society to dominate the discourse, thus discouraging the active participation of representatives of many segments of society that traditionally have little or no voice in the way Honduras is governed. Within weeks and months of the Maduro *Diálogo*, many people were leaving the process or opting not to join it. Most of the leaders of the *Diálogo* sessions were the traditional political heavyweights of the Nationalist Party. This was clearly not going to work because for a national dialogue to be dynamic and successful, it must inspire a wide diversity of people to speak up without concern of being interrupted or fear of being castigated.

A true national dialogue is one where the power players in a society mostly listen, while those who rarely get a chance to talk do the talking. Hopefully, President-elect Porfirio "Pepe" Lobo has learned from the shortcomings of the Maduro *Diálogo*. While Mr. Maduro's concept was good, its implementation was poor – evidenced by the fact that whenever it is mentioned, people either give a questioning look or roll their eyes.

Mr. Lobo's version of the *Gran Diálogo Nacional* commenced only yesterday, so it is too soon to offer a verdict. It is encouraging to see that many sectors of Honduran society are participating, including representatives of the different political parties and institutions within civil society such as churches and non-governmental organizations (NGOs). It is too bad that the one group with whom Mr. Lobo is going to need to reconcile – the National Resistance Front – is opting to stay away from the process. It is tough to have a meaningful *Gran Diálogo Nacional* when a large segment of Honduran society is absent.

Members of *la Resistencia* were invited to be a part of the *Gran Diálogo Nacional*, but apparently they declined. Perhaps they felt their presence might be construed as lending legitimacy to Mr. Lobo, or maybe they simply were not interested because they did not feel anyone would listen. Fair enough. But their absence does nothing to help their cause. While it may be a principled position, it merely serves to isolate them further from the reality of a Lobo government during the next four years, and it makes them appear more radical and unreasonable to a country that has largely decided to move on.

NOTES

We must effectively address poverty in a united manner so that there is no "us" and "them". Whatever strategy is undertaken should be primarily about mobilizing society, inspiring people, and creating a sense of unity.

❈
MORE BLOOD FOR THE HOLIDAYS

December 21, 2009

Many people have expressed concern about the human rights situation in Honduras during the past few months. They are responding to reports from monitoring organizations such as Amnesty International and the Quixote Center that highlight deaths and abuse of people engaged in demonstrations against the interim government of Roberto Micheletti – actions attributed to the security forces. There are multipe sides to many of these stories. Seldom is one side responsible for all the violence and provocations.

The monitoring groups tend to focus on the individuals who have died, been hurt, or disappeared. They see that the police and the soldiers are the ones with the weapons. Meanwhile, the government and its security forces, which consist of individuals drawn from families similar to those of many of the demonstrators, tend to focus on the anger and unpredictability of a large and mobile group of demonstrators, damage to property, and the interruption of daily life for many citizens. What they see is the potential threat of a crowd morphing into an uncontrollable mob. There is ample reason for fear on both sides.

In his letter to President Obama on November 14, Manuel Zelaya noted, "more than 600 people wounded and injured in the hospitals, more than 100 assassinations and an unknown number of people subjected to torture committed against citizens who dare to oppose and express their ideas of liberty and justice in peaceful demonstrations". It is difficult to know the source of these figures or their accuracy, but since Mr. Zelaya has seldom been entirely accurate about anything during the past six months or during his three and a half years in office, some skepticism is justified.

Whether the number of people who have died directly or indirectly as a result of Mr. Zelaya's overthrow is 100 or the more commonly cited 30, it is still a tragedy. But it is important not to lose sight of the reality that this tragedy is only one of many tragedies that continue to occur among the three-quarters of the Honduran population who suffer from poverty and its many ramifications. Honduras suffers from the tragedy of an AIDS epidemic. There is the tragedy of the horrendous abuse of women, children, and homosexuals as a consequence of the disease of *machismo* or narrow-minded morality. There is the tragedy of Honduran fathers and mothers abandoning their families to look for work in the United States.

Obviously, there is the tragedy of a crime situation in Honduras that makes the ousting of a president seem positively tame by comparison. So many people in Honduras die each week from street crime, personal vendettas, gang violence, and institutional negligence that it is easy to become immune to it all.

Perhaps one of the strangest tragedies having to do with human violence in Honduras is the one that is foretold at least twice a year whenever hospitals in the country launch mass blood drives in preparation for a major religious holiday. This happens just before Easter and in the days leading up to Christmas. Public hospitals in Honduras such as the Hospital Escuela in Tegucigalpa and the Hospital Mario Catarino Rivas in San Pedro Sula have now launched blood drives to restock their supplies in anticipation of the spike in accidents and murders that will occur during the upcoming festive season when people drink more and, consequently, get on each other's nerves and fight and argue more.

It is tragically ironic that celebrations honoring an individual whose life was dedicated to teaching people how to love and forgive unconditionally, and thereby discover the secret to living in peace, are accompanied by so much suffering and death. The greater tragedy is that we have somehow grown to accept this as natural and unavoidable, rather than be outraged as we are when we perceive our human rights have been compromised. At a minimum, it's about clinging to some sense of perspective.

NOTES

1.   The level of violence in Honduras has been relatively mild, certainly by world standards. It is also mild compared to the violence that at least 50 percent of the Honduran people face every day of their lives. There is no greater violence toward people than severe poverty... the kind that does not allow parents to feed, clothe, or educate their children; the kind of poverty that diminishes the dignity of individuals; the kind of poverty that makes parents helpless to save their children's lives because they cannot afford the proper medicines or do not have access to a hospital; the kind of poverty that keeps people enslaved and treated as animals. This is the real violence in Honduras that many Hondurans in the middle and upper classes either do not see or choose not to see. Mr. Zelaya is a temporary sideshow, a circus act. Honduras' core problems are still waiting to be addressed, which is why professional diplomats and government officials who are spinning their wheels trying to concoct clever formulas for dealing with the political crisis are missing the point.

2. The question of whether or not there is a conspiracy by the Honduran government to eliminate people who are believed to be a part of the Resistance should be considered in the context of the nature of Honduras. The country is broken. It has dysfunctional institutions, including government, security forces, labor unions, the media, and on and on. It functions poorly in the best of circumstances, so it should come as no surprise to anyone that it would function extremely poorly under the trauma of an overthrow of a president who had already done much to create chaos, fear, hatred, and mistrust within Honduran society. If the military and the police are guilty of beatings, murders and rapes, then this must be addressed. But bickering about the numbers should not be the focus, because numbers are often manipulated.

3. There are and have long been human rights abuses in Honduras. But who is responsible?" The government must accept its share of responsibility. Security forces must accept their share. Those who choose to amass in public and threaten public order, destroy property, and block the right of others to go about their lives in peace must accept their share. Last but not least, Manuel Zelaya must accept his share.

THE DOOMED CAUSES OF RESISTANCE

December 25, 2009

The National Resistance Front Against the Coup d'État formed shortly after Manuel Zelaya was overthrown as president of Honduras on June 28. As its name suggests, the movement adopted as its primary cause the immediate reinstatement of Mr. Zelaya. For more than five months, members of *la Resistencia* marched daily in the streets and demonstrated in parks and in front of government buildings while Mr. Zelaya flew up and down the Western Hemisphere lobbying for support from foreign leaders and then finally opted to sneak back into Honduras and sequester himself in the Brazilian embassy in Tegucigalpa.

Following the election of Porfirio Lobo as president on November 29 and the overwhelming vote on December 2 by Congress to reject Mr. Zelaya's reinstatement, it became clear to *la Resistencia* that it had bet on a losing cause. So *la Resistencia* announced that it would no longer seek Mr. Zelaya's reinstatement but would instead focus its efforts on pushing for the establishment of a National Constituent Assembly, or *la Constituyente*, to better represent the interests of all Hondurans. Now, *la Resistencia* has apparently decided to latch on to the issue of opposing Honduras' withdrawal from the Bolivarian Alliance for the Americas (ALBA) as its cause célèbre.

There is an emerging pattern to the causes that *la*

Resistencia chooses to adopt, and that is that they all appear to be struggles with little or no chance of success. There is nothing wrong with fighting for causes where the odds of winning seem insurmountable. In fact, there is often something noble about unwinnable causes... so long as the causes themselves are noble.

Fighting for the reinstatement of a democratically elected president who was removed from power at gunpoint and illegally taken to a foreign country without even so much as due process is a noble cause. Fighting to create a new legislative body that is less corrupt than an existing one and represents a wider swath of the country's population is a noble cause. Both of these struggles may go nowhere and all that would have been accomplished in the end was to have taken a principled stand to make a point, but still you might say that it was worth the effort.

There is nothing noble about fighting to remain in an economic and political alliance led by countries (Venezuela and Cuba) headed by individuals who possess dictatorial powers and gigantic egos, oversee socialist economies that are in disarray, and severely repress the freedoms and entre-preneurial spirit of their fellow citizens. The models represented by these countries espouse nothing particularly just, innovative or socially progressive in the history of the world – much less anything noble or economically successful.

Once again, *la Resistencia* has bet on a losing proposition and may be at risk for squandering yet more of the public attention and support that it initially attracted. When you pick three consecutive losers, even your fans begin to grumble and fade away.

NOTES

1. Mel seems willing to give up the idea of a National Constituent Assembly in exchange for his reinstatement. It would be more impressive if he were willing to give up his reinstatement in exchange for establishing a National Constituent Assembly. This would at least suggest that he truly is more concerned about the people than about himself.

2. It is unfortunate that *la Resistencia* has placed so much of its hopes on Mr. Zelaya. Mel's promises have always represented a false hope to the people of Honduras because they originated primarily from his grandiose desires and need to be loved. The people in *la Resistencia* are involved in an honorable struggle to alter the imbalances that exist in Honduran society. They are courageous and committed, and they deserve to be taken seriously.

3. *La Resistencia* would do itself a tremendous service if its participants considered leaving their Venezuelan flags at home. If anything, invoking the spirit of Hugo Chávez diminishes their legitimacy, creates more fear, and reinforces the feeling within a huge segment of Honduran society that getting rid of Mr. Zelaya was the right thing to do. It is akin to carrying the Confederate flag down a street in Harlem or the south side of Chicago.

MAXIMUM PRAGMATISM ON MINIMUM WAGE

December 28, 2009

One of Manuel Zelaya's most controversial moves while he was president was to issue a decree to increase the minimum wage by 60 percent in January 2009, from Lps 3,428 ($181) per month to Lps 5,500 ($289.47) per month. Now that Mr. Zelaya is out of power, it is possible that the decree will be overturned, and so there are already whispers on the street about how much of a reduction in the minimum wage Honduran workers would be willing to accept. According to José Luis Baquedano, who heads the United Confederation of Workers in Honduras (CUTH), his union will propose a minimum monthly salary of Lps 8,500, or about $450. Mr. Baquedano notes that this would be just enough to cover basic living requirements such as healthcare, housing, education, and the cost of public services.

If you possess even a rudimentary grasp of mathematics, you can see this is headed straight to another labor strike. Mr. Zelaya had it right about the need to significantly raise the minimum wage. The problem is that he increased it in a unilateral manner, without reaching a negotiated agreement with the business community in Honduras. Mr. Zelaya argued that he tried to negotiate in good faith, but that business leaders kept dragging their feet... and besides, the minimum wage had not been raised for years and workers were no longer able to pay for even the basic necessities of life.

It is possible to sympathize with Mr. Zelaya's intentions but, because of his clumsy and dictatorial style of governing, he ended up hurting the people he was trying to help more than had he tried harder to reach a consensus with the business associations on a more moderate wage rise. Many people lost their jobs because businesses could not afford to pay the higher wage and keep all their employees. And more people lost their jobs because of the political crisis that ensued during the second half of the year, caused in part by the shock of the 60 percent hike and the bad feelings that it created between Mr. Zelaya and business leaders.

Now Mr. Zelaya is gone, and labor leaders in Honduras are going to have to deal with a president from the conservative Nationalist Party. The minimum wage that Mr. Zelaya forced through may not stand. It's a good bet that the Lobo administration will propose a minimum wage of something in between the previous Lps 3,428 per month and the current Lps 5,500. If labor adopts Mr. Baquedano's proposed Lps 8,500, then obviously they are going to have to close a huge gap in order to reach a deal.

Thousands of workers may be striking on the streets of Tegucigalpa and San Pedro Sula before next summer. Clearly, that will cost Honduras yet more millions of dollars in lost business and lost opportunities. So it behooves President-elect Lobo to start talking behind the scenes with labor leaders to begin negotiating a compromise. It is going to have to be less than Mr. Zelaya's magic Lps 5,500, but perhaps not too much less... for the pure sake of pragmatism, not to mention national reconciliation.

NOTES

Workers in Honduras get paid very little. Even worse, they

often do not get paid consistently or in full, and so they are forced to spend an inordinate amount of their time, energy and emotional capital fighting for what is owed them.

ODD ODYSSEY FOR MARTYRDOM

December 30, 2009

Manuel Zelaya's odd odyssey following his ousting on June 28 will likely end in the Brazilian embassy. There is no urgency for Mr. Zelaya to leave the embassy and seek asylum in a foreign country before January 27, 2010 when his term of office will, as he sees it, "officially expire". In fact, it is becoming clear that what Mr. Zelaya is aiming for is the ultimate effect... to go down in history as a martyr.

Now that he has blown his chance at a long-term presidency, like that of Hugo Chávez who is closing out his 11th year as president of Venezuela, Mr. Zelaya will grasp for the next best thing within reach. As Adam Isacson of the Center for International Policy in Washington, DC was recently quoted in *America* magazine, "He seems to be going for martyrdom".

Although Mr. Zelaya has failed at everything he has attempted to do to regain power and has faded from the international headlines, he remains either a strange curiosity or a legendary figure for many, and so it is probably in his best interest, from an image standpoint, to wait it out in the Brazilian embassy and try to claim some sort of victory. He will say, for example, that he outlasted the *golpistas* and refused to negotiate with them, defiant until the end. He will say that he stayed true to his principles and never backed down, maintaining his dignity and honor. He will say that he selflessly sacrificed himself and endured untold hardship, imprisoned for the sake of the Honduran people and for democracy.

Many people might find it difficult to keep a straight face in the midst of this surreal comedic drama, but beware: like it or not, there will be two histories written about Mr. Zelaya. The one that will predominate will be the one written by the winners, as is always the case. But there will be another history that will persist for a time, and that is the one that is being carefully orchestrated during these final weeks in the Brazilian embassy in Tegucigalpa.

The photos of Mr. Zelaya playing his guitar with his daughter, "La Pichu", and singing revolutionary songs dedicated to the *golpistas* were not random. Neither was Mr. Zelaya's announcement that he and his family would spend Christmas Eve eating tamales and praying for presidents throughout the Americas, that they not have to suffer being overthrown by coups. Neither were Mr. Zelaya's passing revelations that he received thousands of handmade Christmas cards from Hondurans and calls from international leaders wishing him well. It is all very romantic. It stirs the emotions.

Some 200 supporters of Mr. Zelaya gathered last night near the Brazilian embassy for a candlelight vigil in a show of solidarity with, in the words of activist Nora Miselem, "the legitimate president of the Honduran people". "I've come because the only true icon that we have in Honduras is 'Mel' Zelaya" said Carlos Barahona. The "Mel as icon and martyr" version is every bit as true for those who experience it as the one that paints the man in a much less favorable light is to others. Hondurans will have to find a way to reconcile these two divergent realities of history.

DEMOCRACY IS HOLLOW
WITHOUT FOOD TO EAT

December 31, 2009

In the weeks following the overthrow of Manuel Zelaya as president of Honduras, there were mass rallies of 50,000 to 100,000 people in Tegucigalpa and San Pedro Sula in favor of peace and democracy. The events were organized by the Civic Democratic Union. There were also massive demonstrations in those cities in favor of democracy and the reinstatement of Mr. Zelaya. Those protests were organized by the National Resistance Front Against the Coup d'État. The common thread was democracy, although of course each side held its own unique interpretation of the meaning of that concept.

But democracy really only means something to those who possess the most basic means of survival... like food and water. The ideal somehow rings hollow, without any practical or philosophical significance, to someone who is desperately scavenging for crumbs and drops so that they and their children can simply exist for one more day. For such people, democracy is an irrelevant luxury. For them, political arguments about coups, the Constitution, Mel, the threat of Hugo Chávez, the wisdom of US policy, and qualifying for the World Cup must seem painfully surreal. As the 18th century British journalist William Cobbett observed, "Without bread all is misery".

It has not rained for four months in much of Honduras. In

the southern half of the country, 90 percent of the crops have been lost and drinking water is becoming increasingly scarce, to the point where people are drinking even more contaminated water than usual, creating the threat of outbreaks of a wide assortment of deadly diseases, including cholera. The government has now declared a state of emergency in Tegucigalpa due to the extremely low levels of the city's two main water reservoirs. Some 300,000 families in the south are struggling to find enough food and water. The UN is warning that 100,000 people in Honduras may soon find themselves at risk for famine.

Are you paying attention? This is serious stuff.

When Hondurans witnessed the outpouring of nationalism, patriotism, and a spirit of camaraderie this past summer and then again in the weeks leading up to the election on November 29, many felt that this was symbolic of some sort of transformation that was occurring within the Honduran psyche... that suddenly we had been awakened to the preciousness of this thing called democracy and that we would no longer take it for granted. There was a vague idea that Hondurans would now put aside their defective tradition of apathy and become personally involved in changing Honduras into a more just, equitable, and compassionate society.

So here we stand in the midst of an evolving food crisis that is already exacerbating malnutrition among tens of thousands of our fellow citizens and is threatening to become a full-fledged famine unless someone does something to prevent it. Unfortunately, the temptation within Honduran society is to assume that it is the responsibility of government to respond to the situation, with the support of international aid organizations and the charity of foreign governments.

Where did all the enthusiasm generated by the masses of people in the streets and parks throughout Honduras mobilized to demonstrate for peace and democracy during the political crisis go? Why is it missing now that we have a food crisis? Perhaps it is just a lack of awareness or, more cynically, a lack of interest. Either way, we have to find it and mobilize it for this new cause because it is the right thing to do, but also because if we don't then we have been fooling ourselves into believing that we are better and more enlightened now than we were before June 28, 2009.

NOTES

1. The biggest threat to Honduras are not the "*Melistas*" or "*golpistas*" or any "*istas*" in between. The biggest threat to Honduras is the status quo and the possibility that there remains too much apathy to change so that the majority of its people do not have to worry about where their next meal will come from, where they will find shelter, or how they will clothe, educate or cure their children.

2. A large portion of Honduras' population has always felt that their rights are constantly minimized because of the extreme social and economic inequities. What good is having the right to vote for either the Blue or Red candidate on the ballot when, either way, your life is not going to substantially change? Mel's promises, even though they may have been empty promises, looked very attractive to the poor because they gave them hope that their lot in life would improve.

3. A more important factor than economic growth for providing core things such as education and healthcare is inspired leadership and mobilization of citizen action. This is an ideal worth working towards. The largest budget item in the Honduran national budget is education. Yet Hondurans are among the most poorly educated people in the world. More money is not going to solve this problem. It is the same

with healthcare. You do not need much money to be healthy. You need to be well-informed and have the ability to make good choices. The US spends the most per capita on healthcare of any nation in the world, yet it is one of the least healthy nations. In Honduras, more than half of the health problems could be resolved by simply providing clean drinking water.

Trading Power for Reconciliation

January 6, 2010

It is ironic that the person to whom President-elect Porfirio Lobo owes the largest debt of gratitude for his election is the same person from whom he now needs to completely disassociate himself. Were it not for the backbone, adequate diplomatic skill, and overall steady hand demonstrated by interim president Roberto Micheletti during the tumultuous months following the overthrow of Manuel Zelaya, it is likely that the elections on November 29 may not have gone so successfully, and thus may not have been recognized by the United States and a few other countries.

Without this recognition, Mr. Lobo would find himself in an infinitely more difficult situation. It is even possible that had it not been for Mr. Micheletti's resolve against international pressure to reinstate Mr. Zelaya that the deposed president may have found himself back in power and cleverly arranged to have the elections postponed – a delay that could have given Mr. Zelaya time to manipulate events to allow for the rewriting of Honduras' Constitution to enable him to run for a second presidential term.

So it is entirely understandable that many people are upset at Mr. Lobo for insisting that Mr. Micheletti step down from power prior to inauguration day so that the new administration can avoid even a perception of approval for or transitional ties to the old administration associated with Mr.

Zelaya's ousting. A whiff of ingratitude, even betrayal, may follow Mr. Lobo around for a long time. While some in Honduras will continue to view Mr. Micheletti negatively because of his role in what many believe was a coup d'état, at least as many will assign to Mr. Micheletti near-iconic status for helping save Honduras from a socialist dictatorship closely allied with and indebted to Hugo Chávez.

It is also reasonable to feel anger toward the US State Department, which has Craig Kelly and other diplomats working behind the scenes to exert pressure and conjure up palatable scenarios for ensuring that there is some sort of space between the end of the Micheletti government and the beginning of Mr. Lobo's. By creating distance between the two, the latter can have a chance at starting fresh without being overly tainted by its proximity to the former. Without at least an appearance of disassociation from the Micheletti government, the Lobo administration will stand little chance of quickly normalizing relations with traditional friends such as Spain and Brazil, along with the vast majority of countries in the Western Hemisphere.

In the midst of all these feelings, it is important to remember that there is at stake here an issue larger than gratitude or some sense of fairness toward Mr. Micheletti. There remains an agreement known as the Tegucigalpa-San José Accord that has yet to be fully implemented by those representing Mr. Micheletti and Mr. Zelaya. The agreement was signed by both parties on October 30, and one of its key terms calls for the formation of a Government of Unity and National Reconciliation. It is precisely that provision that is at the center of efforts by Mr. Lobo and the State Department to have Mr. Micheletti step aside sooner rather than later.

The problem with the provision dealing with the government of reconciliation – as with most of the provisions of the Tegucigalpa-San José Accord – is that it does not specify who is supposed to head the government. Mr. Zelaya assumed that he would lead it, while Mr. Micheletti always assumed he would. In their haste to come up with a signed agreement, negotiators for Mr. Micheletti and Mr. Zelaya, pressured by the US government, simply assigned responsibility for ironing out the details for implementing the agreement to a so-called Verification Commission.

That commission, which consists of Zelaya adviser Jorge Arturo, Micheletti adviser Arturo Corrales, former Chilean president Ricardo Lagos, and US Secretary of Labor Hilda Solis, still exists and maintains responsibility for implementing the agreement. The commission has failed to come up with a plan for a reconciliation government that is acceptable to both Mr. Micheletti and Mr. Zelaya, but the process remains in effect. What Mr. Lobo and the State Department are doing is trying to jumpstart it.

It is tempting to want to forget about the Tegucigalpa-San José Accord and write it off as merely a maneuver to get the US to recognize the elections, particularly since Mr. Zelaya wrote off the agreement a long time ago. Given Mr. Lobo's resounding electoral win, US recognition of the results, and Congress's overwhelming rejection of Mr. Zelaya's reinstatement, it is convenient to treat the agreement as no more than an afterthought now that Honduras is only three weeks away from inauguration day and the drama of Mr. Zelaya is fast fading. That would be a mistake.

The idea of a Government of Unity and National Reconciliation is a good one. Originally, it was meant to bring the opposing factions together to help usher in a period of calmness leading up to the elections so that they could be conducted in a peaceful, transparent and participatory manner. Even without a reconciliation government in place, the elections managed to proceed smoothly enough to gain the support of some of the countries that matter most to the development and stability of Honduras, but not enough to attract the backing of many others that are nearly as vital.

If, by establishing a very brief transitional government of reconciliation led by someone seen as more neutral than Mr. Micheletti, Honduras can provide countries such as Spain and Brazil (and most members of the OAS) with the political cover their governments require to recognize the Lobo government without looking to their constituencies as if they're back-pedaling, then it might be worth the price of appearing ungrateful to Mr. Micheletti. After all, in the end it is not about what is best for any one individual, but rather what is in the interest of the country as a whole.

In addition to his stubborn strength, Mr. Micheletti has displayed a tremendous degree of dignity and selflessness throughout Honduras' political crisis. Mr. Micheletti offered on countless occasions to relinquish power if Mr. Zelaya would agree to give up his claim to the presidency and stop inciting people to insurrection. During the days just prior to and after the elections, he willingly removed himself from the day-to-day operations of the government and accepted a low visibility role in order to allow citizens to focus on the electoral process without being distracted. It would not be surprising to see Mr. Micheletti put aside his ego in a similar fashion sometime in the next week or two.

NOTES

Mr. Micheletti has wisely decided to adopt a low profile. Silence will help solidify Mr. Micheletti's reputation as a serious person who performed the job he was asked to do by Congress and then quietly retired without a lot of fanfare. The contrast between Mr. Micheletti and Mr. Zelaya could not be greater.

Pepe's Bewildering Invitation

January 8, 2010

Some may view President-elect Porfirio Lobo's acknowledgment earlier this week that he has invited all presidents, including Hugo Chávez of Venezuela and Daniel Ortega of Nicaragua, to attend his upcoming inauguration with a mix of suspicion, bewilderment, and distaste. After all that Honduras has done over the past six months to try and rid itself of the influence of these meddlesome, troublesome, and insulting individuals, what in the world could Pepe be thinking? The reasonable thing would be to place Mr. Chávez and Mr. Ortega on Honduras' list of *personae non gratae* and not invite them to the party.

The short explanation for Mr. Lobo's open and conciliatory attitude toward Mr. Chávez and Mr. Ortega is that Pepe realizes that he has to govern as a strong leader and thus that he must refuse to be handicapped by fear, intimidation, and feelings of resentment. There is absolutely no reason why Honduras cannot have diplomatic and commercial relations with countries like Venezuela, Nicaragua, and all the other ALBA countries, including Cuba. And no reason why Honduras cannot have relations with Iran or North Korea.

There is nothing inherently wrong or unwise about engaging people or countries that may represent a threat. If the threat is real, then it is unlikely to simply fade away through timid responses. Engaging, rather than retreating, may be the wiser course.

Mr. Lobo is a seasoned politician. He appears to have an abundance of confidence in himself and has no problem speaking his mind. He has a black belt in karate. He supports the death penalty. He is from Olancho – Honduras' equivalent of the American Wild West. Pepe is no shrinking violet.

Mr. Lobo won his election with a resounding 56 percent of the popular vote. He believes he has a mandate to unite Hondurans and move boldly to deal with Honduras' many problems, and he realizes that he must begin his administration by at least trying to get along with everyone from the outset. If he cannot make it work with Mr. Chávez and Mr. Ortega on his own terms, then one would surmise he will deal with it at the appropriate time.

In his acceptance speech after winning the presidency, Mr. Lobo forcefully stated, "Honduras is a free, independent and sovereign country... we will not allow anyone's interference nor political compromises that may create division." The words were clearly aimed at Mr. Chávez.

All Mr. Lobo is doing by displaying a willingness to receive heads of state who are dangerous and distrustful (not to mention tediously verbose and annoying) is keeping all of his options open. The key is for Pepe to remember that he always maintains the word "no" in his vocabulary, and that he is free to occasionally take it out, dust it off, and use it.

THE CYNICISM OF HONDURAN RECONCILIATION

January 12, 2010

Time is quickly running out for the idea of setting up a Government of Unity and National Reconciliation. It's just as well. The idea was poorly conceived in the first place, and efforts to try and implement it have been pitiful. The only ones who really want such a transitional lame duck body in place before January 27 when President-elect Porfirio Lobo is scheduled to be inaugurated is Mr. Lobo and the US State Department.

And it seems like the only reason Mr. Lobo supports it is because the State Department wants it. And the State Department wants it because it is specified in the Tegucigalpa-San José Accord that the US has touted as a diplomatic victory. Without a Government of Unity and National Reconciliation in Honduras within the next week or two, there will be no way to regard the Tegucigalpa-San José Accord as anything other than what it is: a hollow deal.

The signing of the Tegucigalpa-San José Accord by representatives of interim president Roberto Micheletti and deposed president Manuel Zelaya on October 30 did manage to create at least a perception that the opposing sides in Honduras' then five-month political crisis were on their way to making up. It created hope that Hondurans could begin to let bygones be bygones and commence mending the tears in the fabric of their society. The agreement began to fall apart within days of its signing because it was too vaguely worded and thus overly subject to misinterpretation, but it allowed the US government enough wiggle room for some clever diplomatic maneuvering.

Less than a week after the signing, US Assistant Secretary of State for Western Hemisphere Affairs Thomas Shannon, who played a key role in getting the two sides to make a deal, declared it an historic agreement and said that now it was up to the Honduran people. He held up the document as proof that Hondurans were ready to move forward in peace and thus as a sign that the upcoming elections on November 29 were worthy of recognition and support by the US and the international community.

Mr. Shannon's eagerness to publicly announce that the US would back the elections before waiting to gauge the true level of commitment from each side to implement the Tegucigalpa-San José Accord effectively doomed the agreement. From that moment on, Mr. Zelaya and his supporters knew they had lost because there was no longer any incentive for Mr. Micheletti or the Honduran Congress to act.

Mr. Shannon's remarks in favor of the elections took tremendous pressure off the Micheletti government and elated a sizable portion of Honduras' population that had feared the consequences of continued economic isolation from the US, as well as the demoralizing effect of feeling abandoned by a powerful friend and ally. Mr. Shannon's remarks had the opposite impact of deflating the hopes of Mr. Zelaya and his supporters.

By eliminating all uncertainty surrounding its support for the elections, the US gave the Micheletti government, Honduran society, and many international observers what they needed to participate with confidence and enthusiasm in the electoral process, thus helping ensure its success. While there is some doubt as to the exact level of turnout by eligible voters, it appears that the election drew in the range of 45-60 percent. But the key is that the process was conducted in an orderly, transparent, and relatively peaceful manner. This further diminished any urgency for implementing the Tegucigalpa-San José Accord, particularly the provision calling for a Government of Unity and National Reconciliation.

On December 2, the Congress voted 111-14 to reject reinstating Mr. Zelaya as president. The Tegucigalpa-San José Accord gave Congress the authority to decide Mr. Zelaya's fate. Had Congress been faced with chaos on the streets of Honduras' cities and uncertainty about US policy toward Honduras, it may have struggled with how to come down on the issue of reinstatement. The successful election and the new positive US position made the vote easy for most members of Congress. It is at that point that the political rationale for a Government of Unity and National Reconciliation disappeared for the Micheletti government.

With relative peace and stability in the streets, renewed US support, a newly-elected president, a diffused Resistance movement, and a less vocal Mr. Zelaya still sequestered in Brazil's embassy, what practical reason was there for a Government of Unity and National Reconciliation? From the perspective of the Micheletti government, there was none because the main objective of a Government of Unity and National Reconciliation – a successful election recognized by the US – was fulfilled.

For the Micheletti government, the Tegucigalpa-San José Accord has been a boon. For the US, the agreement has served its purpose. It has allowed the US to play the role of peacemaker and help keep the lid on the political crisis in Honduras, while continuing to take a "principled" stand against what it and most countries around the world view as a coup d'état. Keeping Hugo Chávez in a ranting and bewildered state of "check" has been icing on the cake.

However, in order to show that it was sincere about the Tegucigalpa-San José Accord, the US must continue pushing for its full implementation. That is why two weeks shy of Mr. Lobo's inauguration, the US still insists on a Government of Unity and National Reconciliation, even though neither Mr. Micheletti nor Mr. Zelaya (nor for that matter, most Hondurans) have the faintest interest in it. Sure, everyone embraces the ideals. But true unity and reconciliation are not as simple as that, and Honduras is nowhere close.

ÓSCAR ARIAS SNUBS HONDURAS... AGAIN

January 14, 2010

President Óscar Arias of Costa Rica holds an awfully big grudge against Honduras. It seems like every time he opens his mouth he comes up with a more creative and bizarre way to belittle something or someone in the country. Back in September, Mr. Arias said that he thought Honduras' Constitution was the worst in the world. What? Worse than North Korea's? Worse than Cuba's? Pick a theocracy in the Middle East or Asia. Pick a nation embroiled in genocide or civil war in Africa. Come on buddy... get real.

Now, Mr. Arias is saying that he will not attend the upcoming inauguration of President-elect Porfirio Lobo because of Mr. Lobo's inability to convince interim president Roberto Micheletti to step down and make way for a neutral government of reconciliation that would add legitimacy to the election of November 29, thus allowing more international officials and heads of state to be present on January 27. He criticizes Mr. Lobo for this "weakness". Uh... what?

This is coming from a man who tried for weeks in July to help mediate the evolving political crisis in Honduras shortly after the ousting of Manuel Zelaya, and failed miserably? Mr. Arias, who has been living off his reputation as a topnotch peacemaker after winning the Nobel Peace Prize in 1987 for his work in negotiating an end to the Central American conflicts of the 1980s, was unable to arrive at a settlement that the opposing sides in Honduras could support and sign. He was roundly criticized in Honduras for the extreme bias and lack of public discretion that he displayed from the outset of the talks in Costa Rica. Mr. Arias was never even able to get Mr. Micheletti and Mr. Zelaya to meet face to face, which showed the limitations of Mr. Arias' stature and doomed the process.

It must have rankled Mr. Arias to no end that the beautiful plan he methodically devised was repeatedly rejected. It seemed like a perfectly reasonable and well-crafted peace plan, so he could not bring himself to comprehend what was wrong with it. Ultimately, Mr. Arias decided that the problem was not his plan but rather Mr. Micheletti's unwillingness to cooperate, and he said so publicly.

In the end, elements of the "Arias Peace Plan" were considered during the *Diálogo Guaymuras* and incorporated into the Tegucigalpa-San José Accord signed in Tegucigalpa (not in San José) on October 30. It was not lost on Mr. Arias that he received precious little credit for all the time, effort, and personal reputation he invested. The thought of a second Nobel Peace Prize must have entered his mind at one point, particularly given the relatively mild competition for the award last year, as evidenced by President Obama's win.

So it seems that Honduras will forever be the target of Mr. Arias' resentment. He will be a no-show at the inauguration ceremony, which is probably for the best. He did not earn his second peace prize, but he is fast racking up the unpopularity points in Honduras. He will not be greatly missed.

THE GLARING ABSENCE OF CARLOS FLORES

January 16, 2010

It is unusual to find someone in Honduras who has not espoused a point of view or carved out a position on the ousting of Manuel Zelaya. It is particularly unusual to identify a major political, religious, business, or labor leader in Honduras who has not voiced his or her opinions. The same is true for prominent people in the media, arts and entertainment industries.

Former president Ricardo Maduro has been quoted regularly by the press on the issue, as has Cardinal Óscar Andrés Rodríguez, human rights commissioner Ramón Custodio, businessman Adolfo Facussé, novelist Roberto Quesada, and many others. Very few have opted to remain publicly silent and on the sidelines on the matter of Mr. Zelaya. Perhaps the most glaring example of a major leader in Honduras who has opted for this quiet path is former president Carlos Flores Facussé.

Mr. Flores was president of Honduras during 1998-2002. He has long been, and continues to be, a powerful and respected force in Honduran political circles, especially within the Liberal Party from which he hails. He is one of the most seasoned politicians in Honduras, and arguably possesses more gravitas than anyone else in the country just on the merits of his tough, mature leadership during Hurricane Mitch and the immediate aftermath. Mr. Flores is often mentioned as someone who works behind the scenes to make things happen within the Liberal Party. Unlike Mr. Zelaya, Mr. Flores has an economy with words and appearances that has the effect of making people from all sectors of Honduran society take him seriously.

It is actually not all that surprising that Mr. Flores has been extremely low-key during the past six months. Politically, it has allowed him to avoid being labeled too obviously as a *Zelayista* or a *golpista*, thus allowing him to maintain a certain stature within both camps. I suspect that the low public profile of Mr. Flores' daughter, Lizzy, is no mere coincidence either. Lizzy Flores is the Vice-President of the Congress. There has been little or no mention of her in the newspapers for months.

In an interview last week with *La Tribuna* newspaper, interim president Roberto Micheletti was asked about Mr. Flores' absence. Mr. Micheletti noted that Mr. Flores has been disconnected from his administration, and that he (Micheletti) has had no contact with the former president since the day Mr. Zelaya was overthrown. Mr. Micheletti said that Mr. Flores was not in favor of getting rid of Mr. Zelaya by force, and that on several occasions he tried to sway Mr. Zelaya against moving forward with *la cuarta urna* and his efforts to establish a National Constituent Assembly. Mr. Flores apparently warned Mr. Zelaya that what he was doing was unconstitutional and wrong, but Mr. Zelaya would not listen.

Although some may be critical of Mr. Flores for not taking a clear public stance within the political crisis in Honduras, it is as a testament to Mr. Flores' savvy that he chose to step back from the political fracas. He must have figured it was a no-win situation and that nothing he was bound to say or do would make much of a difference anyway. Better to wait until the dust clears, and then see how to play a positive role. Mr. Micheletti described Mr. Flores as a "man of peace" – someone who is always "looking for tranquility".

So it does not sound as if Mr. Micheletti holds any grudges against Mr. Flores. Given Mr. Flores' known opposition to the overthrow of Mr. Zelaya and the distance that he has managed to keep from the interim government, it is possible that, despite his ownership of *La Tribuna* (which has not been overly kind to Mr. Zelaya) and suspicions by the *Zelayistas* about his role in the overthrow, Mr. Flores may have escaped full branding as a *golpista*. This bodes well for Mr. Flores and Honduras, which unfortunately is running short on individuals who are even remotely acceptable to all sides.

OUR FASCINATION WITH SAVIORS

January 17, 2010

Those who have avidly supported Manuel Zelaya during the past six months have done so in a way that almost seems like idol worship, as if the man can say or do no wrong, as if he alone holds all the answers to Honduras' problems, as if he is the savior for whom the Honduran people have long been waiting. Many people in the United States have treated President Obama in a similar fashion. It appears that now many are succumbing to the temptation of doing the same with Roberto Micheletti.

Honduran society should be looking for ways to reconcile itself in the post-Zelaya period and finding ways to unite those who have been on opposite sides of the political crisis, instead of undertaking gestures to show its appreciation to Mr. Micheletti for his resolute leadership as interim president. A boulevard in San Pedro Sula was inaugurated last week in honor of Mr. Micheletti. It was named, "Roberto Micheletti Baín". The Civic Democratic Union (UCD) is preparing an event on Monday in front of the *Casa Presidencial* to honor Mr. Micheletti for "his efforts in defense of democracy in Honduras". The National Association of Industrialists (ANDI) has conferred the title of "First National Hero of Honduras in the 21st Century" to Mr. Micheletti.

Last week, Congress approved a decree to pay Mr. Micheletti a salary for the rest of his life. On top of that,

Congress decorated Mr. Micheletti with its Grand Cross Extraordinaire With Gold Plaque (no doubt a prestigious award) for his years of public service.

These gestures can be irritating and provocative if you're on the other side of an argument.

All this is not about Mr. Micheletti. The man has done an incredible job of holding Honduras together during one of the most difficult times in its history. He has been strong and steady during a period when the country needed such a leader. Unlike Mr. Zelaya, Mr. Micheletti has shown no inclination to remain in power past the point that Congress assigned to him. So notwithstanding Evo Morales' recent comparison to Augusto Pinochet, Mr. Micheletti is no Pinochet... or Chávez, Ortega, or Castro, for that matter.

We seem to put our politicians, clerics, soldiers, or sages on pedestals, and spend our precious time building these pedestals, rather than putting our social houses in order. While some engage in activities to honor Mr. Micheletti and others continue to promote Mr. Zelaya as some sort of martyr, there are more than 300,000 families in the southern half of Honduras who are having a really hard time finding enough food to eat and water to drink due to the drought that has now gone on for nearly five months. The United Nations (UN) is predicting that more than 100,000 people may soon be at risk for famine in Honduras. Somewhere, we have managed to get our priorities all messed up.

The best thing that human beings can do is point the way to a better way of living, and inspire others through their words and personal example. People should not be worshipped, because worship does nothing other than distract from the hard work of transforming ourselves so that we can then go out and change our communities and eventually our nations. Honoring or paying homage to someone may seem normal and fine, but it often has the effect of blinding us and making us apathetic to the needs of those around us. It is very easy to worship. We humans are good at that.

NOTES

Where are the visionary leaders of Honduras? The ones who do not see themselves as saviors, or messiahs. The ones whose self-confidence emanates from humility rather than pride. The ones who want to listen deeply rather than talk endlessly. The ones whose primary goal is not winning but rather offering an example all Hondurans would want to emulate. The ones who will lead by inspiration rather than manipulation.

THE POLITICS OF PRAGMATISM

January 21, 2010

Even though at some level there exists at least a grudging realization among most people in Honduras that there is a need to heal the divisions fueled by the political crisis of the past year, there remains a disturbing reluctance on the part of many on all sides of the conflict to actually take steps in the direction of national reconciliation (and in some cases even familial reconciliation).

A recent letter written by the former Vice-Minister of Foreign Relations in the Zelaya administration to Cardinal Óscar Andrés Rodríguez continues the ever predictable and thus overly worn diatribe by supporters of Manuel Zelaya against anyone who happens to take a position against him. The sterile, inflammatory, and infantile accusations against the Cardinal in response to his publicly stated positions demonstrate how such conflicts turn personal, and how questioning someone's integrity is used to try and win points.

Sadly, similar tactics have been used by opponents of Mr. Zelaya to try and diminish anyone who views his overthrow as wrong, illegal, or even immoral. If you happen to belong to *la Resistencia*, there must be something wrong with you. You must be a socialist, perhaps a communist, or just a troublemaker. You must have been brainwashed. You must be uneducated. The tendency is to paint with a broad brush. So there can be no middle ground – "Either you're with us or you're against us."

These tactics are unhelpful, and fail to take into account that this entire issue is not black or white. There are people of integrity and brilliance on both sides. There are pros and cons on both sides. The only people who are undoubtedly wrong are those who think one side is completely right and the other side is completely wrong.

Not only are these kind of people wrong, they're going to be relatively useless in the post-Zelaya era, as Honduras tries to regroup and pull itself together to undertake yet another series of attempts to deal with its social and economic problems. They are useless because they will be unable to move forward and leave the past behind. Unfortunately, many of these people will never be able to play a constructive role in bettering Honduras because they are so filled with anger, hatred, suspicions, or desire for revenge... or the sum of all.

In the midst of all this unwillingness to let go and begin the long process of reconciliation in Honduras, it is refreshing to hear President-elect Porfirio Lobo talk about forgiveness and looking toward the future. Mr. Lobo has consistently sounded like a man sincerely interested in letting bygones be bygones, not because he's a nice guy or does not care about the law or justice, but rather because he is a pragmatist, not a populist or an ideologue.

Mr. Lobo knows that he cannot effectively address all the challenges he will face beginning on January 27 unless he unifies the country and remains genuinely open to talking with anyone, and actually listening. His announcement yesterday that he would like to include Mr. Zelaya on an advisory council consisting of former presidents sets precisely the right tone and example.

A Little Room for Dignity

January 21, 2010

Many people in Honduras are upset, even enraged, at President-elect Porfirio Lobo for promising to give Manuel Zelaya safe-passage to travel to the Dominican Republic as a "Distinguished Guest". The concern is three-fold.

First, after all that Honduras has gone through in the past year, there is the image of Mr. Zelaya being received with honors anywhere. There is much support in Honduran society for locking Mr. Zelaya up and throwing away the key. Second, there is the matter of Mr. Zelaya's alleged crimes. People are asking, "What... he's just going to get off without any punishment at all?" Lastly, many are worried about Mr. Zelaya's propensity for making trouble if left unleashed. It is one thing to have Mr. Zelaya leave Honduras under political asylum status, which would deny him the freedom to engage in political activities. It is something else entirely to allow him to roam unrestricted.

But Mr. Lobo has only a slew of unappealing options followed by a collection of slightly less unappealing ones. Mr. Lobo is simply trying to find a way to put the Zelaya saga behind him so that he can get on with the job of governing Honduras and work his way through a complex maze of problems that keep the country from moving forward.

If he is forced to continue dealing with this sideshow, Mr. Lobo will never stand a chance at rebuilding Honduras' economy, creating decent paying jobs for people, properly educating children, fixing the country's broken healthcare system, coming up with alternatives to cutting down the forests and having extractive industries destroy the land and poison its rivers, providing clean drinking water, preventing the impending famine in the south, rehabilitating tens of thousands of gang members, fighting drug traffickers, and changing the culture of *machismo* that leads to the abuse of women and children. It is not a short list.

The point is that continuing to dwell on feelings about Mr. Zelaya is not worth it when there is so much real work to be done. The political crisis during the past year has been a soap opera. It has been tragic, and thus it has been distastefully entertaining and time-consuming. It has been addictive like a drug, and so it is natural to find it difficult to lay aside. To his credit, Mr. Lobo knows that this is precisely what has to be done. He will take a lot of heat for letting Mr. Zelaya off the hook so easily, and that's unfortunate because a little mercy is a relatively small price to pay to be left free to begin cleansing Honduras of the mess left behind.

Mr. Lobo has given his fellow *Olanchano* what he seems to have most wanted since his overthrow on June 28 – a way out that permits him to maintain a sense of dignity. In a culture dominated by *machismo*, the concept of honor is central to the identity of many men. This cannot be ignored or under-estimated because it carries the risk of indefinitely prolonging conflicts that eliminate any hope for reconciliation. Mr. Lobo understands this, which is why he is opting for the moral high ground, even if it doesn't feel that way to some.

MEL THE UNGRATEFUL

January 27, 2010

It is easy to understand and even empathize with Manuel Zelaya for being angry, resentful, and vengeful toward interim president Roberto Micheletti, General Romeo Vásquez, the Supreme Court, the Congress, Cardinal Óscar Rodríguez, and business leaders in Honduras, given that they all either played a role in his overthrow or failed to support his efforts to return to power.

It is much harder to make a good case, however, for why Mr. Zelaya would have overly hard feelings toward President-elect Porfirio Lobo. After all, it was Mr. Lobo who signed the agreement with Dominican President Leonel Fernández to grant safe-passage for Mr. Zelaya to leave his self-imprisonment in the Brazilian embassy in Tegucigalpa and visit the Dominican Republic as nothing less than a "Distinguished Guest". Mr. Lobo did not have to do that, and it did not come without a political price.

It would be reasonable to expect that, at some level, Mr. Zelaya would be grateful and even beholden to Mr. Lobo for the kind gesture of allowing him a dignified exit from the hole he's been living in for the past five months. Not only does he get to avoid being arrested and placed in a real prison, he gets to travel to a nice Caribbean island with President Fernández aboard his private jet. He also gets to bring his family and closest advisers with him. In addition, Mr. Lobo has aggressively pushed Congress to approve an amnesty for Mr. Zelaya's political offenses, which include treason and abuse of power.

You would think that Mr. Zelaya would appreciate Mr. Lobo for trying to get Mr. Micheletti to step down from the presidency before the inauguration. Although it would have been a relatively meaningless move, it would have given Mr. Zelaya some pleasure to see his old nemesis brought down a notch. In the end, you have to assume that Mr. Lobo's lobbying was partly responsible for Mr. Micheletti opting gracefully to not be present at the inauguration ceremony and, in fact, deciding to vacate the *Casa Presidencial* a few days ago.

Mr. Lobo has been nothing if not magnanimous and merciful toward Mr. Zelaya. So you have to wonder what it is about Mr. Zelaya's character that would cause him to want to interfere with his fellow *Olanchano's* inauguration by calling on his followers yesterday to go to Toncontín airport to say goodbye to him on the day that rightfully should belong to Mr. Lobo. Was it just a careless sentimental lapse? Would he not think that a mass of people marching off to the airport would be disruptive, could turn into a mob and potentially end in someone getting hurt or even killed? This would all be done, of course, in the presence of dozens of foreign dignitaries and television crews that might twist scenes in a way that could embarrass Mr. Lobo before he even has a chance to start cleaning up Mr. Zelaya's mess. Was it purely the unrestrainable and gigantic ego of a man who believes that he must always be the center of attention?

Mel has always loved parades. Throughout his shortened presidency, he gallantly rode his fine horses on many festive occasions, even in the midst of massive teacher strikes and other crises that demanded his urgent attention. It may be that Mr. Zelaya does not genuinely want to stick it to Mr. Lobo. It appears that what he wants is simply another parade.

THE WISDOM OF GRACIOUSNESS

January 27, 2010

It is possible that I have written more editorials critical of Manuel Zelaya than perhaps anyone in the world. While I have done my utmost to remain civil and respectful toward the man, I have made no effort to hide my dislike of him and my disdain for his manner of governing, treating people, and creating chaos and division within Honduran society. Mr. Zelaya may have done more harm to Honduras than anyone in history. But while my emotions tell me that this individual should be punished and sent to prison for a very long time, my mind says that pragmatism and compassion must win out.

Mr. Zelaya may have cost me a relationship with a cousin to whom I cannot talk without the conversation quickly deteriorating. The mere mention of Manuel Zelaya makes us both itchy to argue. The situation with Mr. Zelaya has made dialogue with my hippest uncle and one of my hippest aunts (... you know, the kind who you could always talk to without fear of being judged or lectured to when you were a kid) potentially awkward. The same is true for exchanges with a good friend of mine in Tegucigalpa with whom I see eye to eye on nearly everything.

I have few reasons to be generous toward Mr. Zelaya, yet for the sake of Honduras I am extremely pleased that President-elect Porfirio Lobo has found the wisdom and political spine to be both generous and gracious toward this beleaguered man. Mr. Lobo recognizes that the country desperately needs a break from Mr. Zelaya. The circus at the Brazilian embassy has been ongoing since September 21 and the overall "Mel-o-drama" since June 28. But the saga of Mel Zelaya has been around for much longer, and it is time to move on to another episode.

Mr. Lobo will give Mr. Zelaya his letter of safe-passage to travel to the Dominican Republic under the status of "Distinguished Guest". Mr. Zelaya may end up getting off for his alleged crimes, but it is a small price to pay to give Honduras a breather and Mr. Lobo a chance to get on with the job of governing the nation. Gerald Ford got it right when he pardoned Richard Nixon, and Barack Obama got it right when he decided not to play along with calls from Democrats to investigate George W. Bush. No one should ever be above the law. But sometimes you have to accept the lesser of two evils.

Mr. Lobo has said that he would accompany Mr. Zelaya and Dominican President Leonel Fernández to Toncontín airport and give them a nice send-off after he is inaugurated as Honduras' new president. That is a stroke of genius. It shows to Honduras and to the world that Mr. Lobo has no fear and is in control of the situation. It also sends a message to the international community that Honduras is moving on and that it is time for everyone else to finally get over it as well.

Congratulations Mr. Lobo. You have begun your presidency well, setting an example for Hondurans to emulate. It is not always about being right, and there is always more than one way to win.

The Path Not Taken

January 29, 2010

Now that Porfirio Lobo has assumed the Presidency of Honduras and Manuel Zelaya has left for the Dominican Republic, the debate about whether or not Mr. Zelaya should be reinstated is a moot one. We have entered the post-Zelaya period. The primary order of business will now be to unite the country by finding ways for people of different opinions on the political crisis of the past year to talk to and engage with each other in ways that are civil, respectful, and forgiving.

Yet probably for many years to come, the question of whether or not Mr. Zelaya deserved to be overthrown will continue to be a source of intense debate. It is a legitimate debate, and intelligent people will disagree. There is no position that is entirely correct, because it largely depends on assumptions, interpretations, and perspectives. Truth is seldom absolute. It is most often relative. This is certainly true for the downfall of Manuel Zelaya.

The debate about whether there is sufficient justification for the Supreme Court to have ordered the removal from power of President Zelaya, and for almost every institution within Honduran society – including Congress, the Armed Forces, the Attorney General, the Human Rights Commissioner, the business sector, and the Church – to have backed the decision, will be a breath of fresh air and a welcomed relief from the stale and dead end argument of whether it was a *golpe* or not a *golpe*. After all, the point is not so much whether or not it was a *golpe*, but rather whether it was a good *golpe* or a bad *golpe*.

Consider the example of war. Most people in the world – apart from extreme pacifists who are willing to sacrifice their lives and the lives of their loved ones before raising a stick to hurt anyone – believe that there are "just wars" and "unjust wars". Most people will believe, for example, that World War II was a just war. Far fewer people will believe Vietnam was a just war. Although in principle most people probably oppose war, many would be willing to break with that principle in certain scenarios. The same logic should apply to a *golpe*, given that a *golpe* is far less destructive and hideous than any war.

The tricky part for those debating in support of Mr. Zelaya's ousting is that a strong part their justification lies in their assumptions, interpretations, and perceptions of what Mr. Zelaya was in the process of doing and intended to do in the future. While there is material evidence to show (according to the Supreme Court and others) that Mr. Zelaya had broken certain key Articles of the Constitution, and thus had automatically forfeited his presidency, the more popular arguments for getting rid of Mr. Zelaya tend to focus more on his intentions to change the Constitution, set up a National Constituent Assembly, perhaps dissolve the Congress, establish a socialist government allied with Hugo Chávez, and remain in power indefinitely.

Making a case for overthrowing Mr. Zelaya based on what he planned to do is tough. It is like a judge convicting and imprisoning someone based on circumstantial evidence. You cannot know for certain what is in a person's mind. You can only speculate, and that is not enough to condemn someone. That is the problem that the US faced in Iraq. The Bush administration launched an invasion of Iraq based on what it believed Saddam Hussein had in his arsenal and intended to do with that arsenal. This same analogy applies to the ousting of Mr. Zelaya.

We will never know for sure whether Mr. Zelaya deserved to be evicted from the *Casa Presidencial* at gunpoint on June 28, 2009. However, if you've been watching what has been going on in Venezuela during the past few years, and particularly the past week, you will get an idea of where Honduras was likely headed. The socialist dictatorship that Mr. Chávez has put in place is destroying one of the wealthiest and most educated societies in Latin America, not to mention one of the most oil-rich countries in the world.

In Venezuela, everything from North American hotels to French supermarket chains are being nationalized. Banks are under constant threat of takeover. The national currency has been devalued by 50 percent. Television stations have been shut down, and schools and universities are being required to indoctrinate students with the political views of the ruling socialist party. Tens of thousands of people are protesting and rioting in the streets, and students have been killed in confrontations with security forces. Now Mr. Chávez is looking to distract Venezuelans by provoking a war with neighboring Colombia.

The natural warmth and increasingly close political ties between Mr. Chávez and Mr. Zelaya during 2008 and the first half of 2009 were evident for all to see. Mr. Zelaya made no secret of his admiration for Mr. Chávez and his Bolivarian socialist revolution in Venezuela. Mr. Zelaya proudly declared himself a leftist, much in the same way as Mr. Chávez recently came out and shed his socialist affiliation and boldly declared himself to be a full-fledged Marxist.

Mr. Zelaya was well on his way to being indoctrinated and instructed on how to emulate the Venezuelan model. Then, the school year was abruptly shortened. Some will say that this was a good thing. Others will disagree. Keep watching what's going on in Venezuela, and see if that is the path you envisioned for Honduras.

NOTES

Regardless of how you may feel about the ousting of Manuel Zelaya, take a look at what's happening now in Nicaragua (as well as in Venezuela), and you may get a sense of what may have happened in Honduras had Mr. Zelaya been allowed to do as he pleased. Follow President Ortega's moves, particularly how he incites the mobs on the streets to intimidate and create chaos. These are not the actions of a responsible president, but rather those of a dictator who has little concern for the development of his country, and is more interested in amassing personal power and control. There is nothing noble, just and visionary about leaders like Daniel Ortega and Hugo Chávez.

A TRUTH HONDURANS RECOGNIZE

February 8, 2010

Perhaps the most difficult challenge facing the Honduras Truth Commission, led by former Guatemalan Vice-President Eduardo Stein, will be to distinguish between facts and interpretations that have been deemed to be facts. It is precisely this chasm between the "reality" of what led to and happened during the overthrow of Manuel Zelaya and the "perception of reality" of what transpired that divides Honduran society.

For example, it is a fact that President Zelaya was planning to hold a poll to gauge public support for setting up *la cuarta urna* during the elections on November 29 to vote on whether or not to review and rewrite the Constitution. It is also a fact that the Supreme Court ruled the poll to be unconstitutional. But is it a fact that the poll was illegal? It will depend on the Commission's interpretation of the Constitution and also whether it wishes to accept the authority of the Judicial or Executive branch of government in this case.

It is a fact that President Zelaya consistently stated that he had no intention of remaining in power one day longer than his term of office provided. But is it a fact that some of the language he used in his speeches and interviews about establishing a National Constituent Assembly to rewrite the Constitution strongly suggested that he wanted to alter the Constitution to allow for presidential re-election, thus allowing him to run for another term and try to manipulate the system to remain in office indefinitely? It will depend on the Commission's interpretation of Mr. Zelaya's words and actions.

Is it a fact that President Zelaya was increasingly acting like an out-of-control dictator by violating laws such as the one requiring the annual submission of a national budget to the Congress, flagrantly ignoring rulings by the Supreme Electoral Tribunal and the Supreme Court, arbitrarily dismissing military officers, and provoking public confrontations by personally inciting mobs to take to the streets? It will depend on the Commission's interpretation of Mr. Zelaya's words and actions, as well as its interpretation of the extent of presidential powers.

It is a fact that the Supreme Court ordered Honduras' Armed Forces to arrest President Zelaya. It is a fact that the Congress, the Attorney General, the Public Ministry, and the Human Rights Commissioner supported this decision. But is it a fact then that the removal of Mr. Zelaya constituted a military coup d'état? It will depend on the Commission's interpretation of what constitutes a military coup d'état. Would the ousting have been less of a coup had the police arrested Mr. Zelaya? Does it matter more who performed the arrest or who ordered it?

The job that is being given to the Truth Commission is an unenviable one because it is an impossible one. It assumes that you can put together a neat summary of the facts that led to June 28, 2009 and all the events afterward. It assumes that facts are absolute, and therefore so is truth. This assumption may lead commissioners to conclude that most Hondurans will be able to recognize the truth in the conclusions the Commission ultimately presents, so long as it is backed up by enough solid evidence, and that this will facilitate the process of reconciliation in Honduras.

Commissioners should be prepared for the possibility, though, that their version of the facts and the truth may have the unintended effect of re-igniting old anger and grievances that have died down a little with the passing of time. Indeed, the idea of a select group of people putting an official stamp of approval on a set of interpretations and calling them facts for history to judge may be so insulting to people's understanding of their own truth of what happened that it may further aggravate divisions in Honduras rather than help to heal them.

A Measure of Misplaced Patriotism

February 12, 2010

There is a decree before the Honduran Congress to declare June 28, 2009 "Day of the protection of democracy and defense of freedom in the country". The measure, proposed by Congressman Eliseo Mejía Castillo of the department of Cortés, would recognize the date as a working civic holiday. Congressman José Ángel Saavedra of Copán has expressed his opposition to the decree because he believes that it would open up a "huge wound that is beginning to heal". Thank you, Mr. Saavedra, for your dose of sanity and plain old common sense.

President Porfirio Lobo is now emphasizing unity and national reconciliation in Honduras, pushing the creation of a Truth Commission to gather information about the events that led up to and transpired during and since June 28, and trying to convince foreign governments to normalize diplomatic relations with Honduras. About the last thing the country needs is an official holiday glorifying the overthrow of a democratically elected president that has resulted in the loss of lives, the destruction of property, the damaging of relationships with other nations, the deterioration of the national economy, and the marring of Honduras' image abroad.

It may be that Honduras dodged a huge bullet by disrupting a series of events that may have been leading the country toward a long-term socialistic dictatorship akin to what exists in Venezuela. It may be that Honduras preserved its imperfect democracy. Many Hondurans are understandably grateful and relieved, and they should be. But that is not the point.

Mr. Zelaya is gone. There were few, if any, good options for ridding Honduras of this man, other than by force. But it is unwise to publicly celebrate his ousting. There is a significant segment of Honduran society that feels betrayed, insulted, and disempowered by what occurred on June 28. Why would anyone wish to go out of their way to rub it in? It is like deliberately running up the score in a game. It's not only bad form and mean-spirited, but foolish and shortsighted, because by doing so you would provoke a backlash that could well result in more violence, destruction, and instability. Nobody wins. Everybody loses.

Mr. Mejía would do well to reflect a bit on the potential consequences of his thoughtless exercise in nationalism or so-called patriotism. It is irresponsible and sadly misplaced.

THE DEMISE OF RESISTANCE

February 25, 2010

The National Resistance Front Against the Coup d'État in Honduras consists of many good people who sincerely feel that the ousting of Manuel Zelaya was wrong, unconstitutional, and illegal, and have thus felt obliged to exercise their democratic right to organize and protest. While some of the demonstrations have turned violent, caused the destruction of property, and interfered with the rights of others to go about their normal lives, most of them have been peaceful and caused relatively few disruptions in Honduras as a whole.

The problem for the National Resistance Front is that the core reason for its birth has gradually faded and become largely irrelevant to the vast majority of people in Honduras who simply want to return to some semblance of normalcy and get back to work so they can feed their families and educate their children. The election and inauguration of Porfirio Lobo as President, the willingness of Mr. Zelaya to leave the Brazilian embassy in Tegucigalpa for the Dominican Republic without too much fanfare, and the gradual re-establishment of diplomatic relations with the international community (... 29 countries thus far) have contributed to a grudging realization that the battle to reverse the overthrow has been lost.

In short, the National Resistance Front finds itself in the difficult situation of being a movement without a clear cause. It has tried to emphasize other causes such as the fight to establish a National Constituent Assembly to rewrite the Constitution, but that has not gained much traction. It has also tried to adopt other causes such as fighting to keep Honduras within Hugo Chávez's ALBA alliance, but that was a short-lived, dismal effort that failed. As eventually happens with all popular social movements, the National Resistance Front has also started to experience division within its ranks, as some of its leading sympathizers such as César Ham have opted to join the new government to try and change the system from within.

Now, in another attempt to remain even a minimally viable force within Honduran politics, the National Resistance Front has decided to use the education of Honduras' children as a tool to keep the political crisis alive. The leaders of the National Resistance Front, which does not recognize the Lobo administration, have called for a national march on Thursday in support of a return to the constitutional order. Given Mr. Lobo's election and Mr. Zelaya's new life abroad, it is unclear what that means in real life. A "return to the constitutional order" sounds more like a campaign slogan than a serious action item.

The march itself may be fine. However, what the National Resistance Front – which includes key organizers within the teachers unions – has done is call on public school teachers in Honduras to join the march rather than remain in their classrooms teaching their students. It was only last week that the leaders of the teachers unions signed an agreement with the Lobo administration to provide at least 200 days of schooling for the children of Honduras. That agreement will quickly begin to fall apart should teachers obey the call by their union organizers, who have slowly permitted themselves to identify more with the nebulous causes of the National Resistance Front than to the tangible cause of fair pay for teachers.

Ironically, the evolving marriage between the National Resistance Front and the teachers unions may end up contributing to the demise of both entities. Public school teachers in Honduras are not much different from other people in Honduras. They just want to be allowed to do their jobs and receive adequate compensation in a timely and consistent manner. They have had to rely on and trust their union organizers and heed their calls to strike or protest in the hope of attaining more power to negotiate pay and benefits with the government. But this latest call to march by the National Resistance Front has more to do with its own political interests than the interests of the teachers, and so there is a growing sense on the part of teachers that this association between their unions and the National Resistance Front may not be such a good thing, thus eroding support for the association and perhaps even for the unions themselves.

Further, by calling on teachers to leave their classrooms rather than perform the tasks for which they were hired, the National Resistance Front is fueling a perception among Hondurans that it is willing to use Honduras' schoolchildren as pawns in its political movement. That perception cannot strengthen its cause, only weaken it. Whatever success the National Resistance Front has had in building popular support within certain segments of Honduran society is on the verge of being dismantled by a distasteful and poorly conceived strategy of using children as bargaining chips.

NOTES

The assumption is that the people who make up the Resistance movement in Honduras are somehow immune to the same temptations and weaknesses as the elite in Honduras. There is nothing particularly more (or less) noble about the Resistance.

There are many people who are not a part of the Resistance who want just as much to transform Honduras for the better, but they are not willing to trash the entire system and start all over again. That leads to chaos and violence, and those who would primarily suffer (as always) will be the poor. The wealthy would leave the country and take all of their resources with them. The model for Honduras should not be Cuba. In Cuba, they simply replaced one corrupt elite class with another corrupt elite class. The goal should be to inspire a change in attitudes. That requires creative leadership and mobilization of everyone for positive and constructive action.

ORTEGA'S DILEMMA

February 27, 2010

Whether by accident or design, the summit with the presidents of Central America proposed by the US State Department for Friday in Guatemala City is a masterful geopolitical stroke that will both speed up the process of reuniting Honduras with its regional neighbors and force Nicaragua to choose whether it wants to align itself more with Central America or with Hugo Chávez and ALBA, which is more of a South American construct. It is notable that Nicaragua's Daniel Ortega is the only Central American president who has not confirmed he will attend the summit.

One of the items on the summit's agenda is the reintegration of Honduras into the community of the nations of the Americas. Honduras' membership in the Organization of American States (OAS) was suspended shortly after the ousting of President Zelaya on June 28, 2009. However, since the election of Porfirio Lobo as president on November 29 and his inauguration on January 27, the governments of several OAS countries have voiced support for welcoming Honduras back to the fold sooner rather than later.

One of the strongest advocates for Honduras of late has been Costa Rican President Óscar Arias, who is not normally considered to be Honduras' best friend. He has been consistent in his view that it would be a mistake to continue to isolate Honduras, and last week at the Group of Rio Summit in

185

Mexico he expressed his disappointment that President Lobo had not been invited to participate. Even OAS Secretary General José Miguel Insulza has hinted that Honduras' suspension may be overturned as early as June when the OAS General Assembly meets in Lima, Perú.

Coming on the heels of the Group of Rio Summit, the upcoming Guatemala Summit, to which Mr. Lobo has been invited, will help allay the perception that Honduras remains some sort of pariah in Latin America and the Caribbean. It will be an opportunity for Mr. Lobo to be seen shaking hands and rubbing shoulders with US Secretary of State Hillary Clinton and the presidents of Central America, thus accelerating the official acceptance of Honduras. This presents a dilemma for President Ortega, who has repeatedly stated that he will not recognize the Lobo government and normalize relations with Honduras. If Mr. Ortega does not show up for the summit, he, not Mr. Lobo, suddenly begins to look like the odd man out, which only weakens Nicaragua's position in the region. Nicaragua already has to tread carefully when it comes to Honduras because 50 percent of its exports go through Honduran territory and out from its ports.

On the other hand, if Mr. Ortega decides to play along and show up at the summit, he sets himself up to look as if he's backpedaling and betraying his friend Mr. Zelaya, who is starting to get restless sitting around in Santo Domingo. Also, the move could send mixed signals to Mr. Chávez and the other ALBA presidents, initiating some misunderstandings and perhaps even cracks in the alliance.

Mr. Ortega may try to be clever and use the summit to emulate Mr. Chávez's recently stated willingness to recognize the Lobo government so long as Mr. Zelaya is allowed to return to Honduras to play an active political role. But to pull that off without looking whiney, awkward, and obstructive would take the skill of a great statesman, which Mr. Ortega is not.

✠

TEXTBOOK DIPLOMACY

March 5, 2010

Today, former president Manuel Zelaya is in Venezuela meeting with President Hugo Chávez and President Porfirio Lobo is in Guatemala visiting with US Secretary of State Hillary Clinton. In a pitiful display of political paranoia, you have Venezuela's Foreign Minister Nicolás Maduro complaining that Mrs. Clinton's goodwill tour through South and Central America during the past week is an egregious effort to intervene in Latin America and destroy the sense of solidarity that exists among the countries of the region.

In the meantime, the political situation in Honduras has stabilized with the peaceful election and inauguration of Mr. Lobo – both of which were made infinitely more likely by the US-brokered Tegucigalpa-San José Accord between representatives of interim president Roberto Micheletti and Mr. Zelaya. Further, the US has recognized the Lobo administration, restarted its economic and military aid programs, and willingly served as an enthusiastic and powerful advocate around the world for normalizing diplomatic relations with Honduras.

Meanwhile, Mr. Chávez is facing violent demonstrations daily on the streets of Venezuelan cities by tens of thousands of citizens who are wary of their government's continuing march toward an unabashed socialist dictatorship and weary with the growing laundry list of acute economic problems. To make things more embarrassing for him, he is being criticized by regional human rights organizations and free press associations and asked to explain some of his more heavy-handed moves by governments of countries such as France and Spain.

My... how things have changed. It was not that long ago that the Obama administration was being blamed for betraying Honduras by condemning the overthrow of Mr. Zelaya and implementing aid sanctions against the Micheletti government. Seems like only yesterday that the Obama administration was being criticized for colluding with Mr. Chávez in some sort of nefarious conspiracy to destroy democracy in Latin America and install socialist regimes throughout the region. It was not that long ago that experts on Latin America were saying, "I just can't understand what the Obama administration is doing in Honduras". If these people were truly experts they might not agree with the administration's policy, but they should at least be able to analyze it, make some sense of it, and explain it in lay terms to the public. Otherwise, what's the point of being an expert?

In the end, the judgment by many was simply that President Obama was a socialist and secretly an admirer of Mr. Chávez, and thus by definition an enemy of democracy, which explained the US government's unwillingness to recognize and support the Micheletti government.

The idea that the US State Department might actually have intelligent and professional people who know a little about the history of US involvement in Latin America and understand how roused Latin Americans get when the US is perceived as supporting forced removals of freely-elected heads of state tended to be dismissed. The notion that the US might be acting to contain the trauma of what many people in Honduras and Latin America viewed as a coup and thus take away the ability of long-winded, opportunistic troublemakers like Mr. Chávez to paint the US in a poor light (and thereby raise his own regional clout) was disregarded.

By only focusing on the superficial and short-term aspects of the State Department's official policy toward Honduras following Mr. Zelaya's ousting, many people failed to distinguish between tactics and strategy in the game of geopolitics. By attributing the mixed signals that the Obama administration appeared to be sending by supporting Mr. Zelaya (but not too much), many people neglected to consider the importance of nuance in international diplomacy, at least until a situation has been given a chance to evolve and become less muddled.

It is possible that the US merely got lucky in Honduras, and that the relatively bright political outlook that is emerging in the country is occurring in spite of US policy rather than because of it. It is possible that the US is extremely fortunate that Mr. Chávez and Mr. Zelaya now find themselves at a loss as to what to do next, given that their receptive audiences are diminishing. It is also possible that the US played a very good game with the cards it was dealt, and that this is precisely what has led to the growing isolation of these two characters and a calming of the political crisis in Honduras.

NOTES

1. The US government has helped contain the damage caused by the trauma of the ousting of a democratically elected president in Honduras. This has happened through some clever political maneuvering... some of it behind the scenes and some of it in the open. Granted, some of the maneuvering certainly appears unsavory, but that is true for much of foreign policy and power geopolitics.

2. One of the biggest problems with US foreign policy is that there is a tendency to personalize issues and attribute fault to

one person. A great example is Osama bin-Laden. The idea is, "If we can just get Osama, all will be well". This way of thinking is dangerous because it denies the reality of why bin-Laden is so popular in the Arab world... just like blaming US ambassador Hugo Llorens denies the reality of why Honduras is in such a mess.

3. Scapegoating is not a useful exercise because it siphons energy and attention from the real causes of the problems of Honduras. It assumes that if the scapegoat were to go away, the problems would also go away or eventually resolve themselves. Scapegoating is primarily done when people have no good answers to problems. It also encourages apathy by encouraging people to think, "Hey, I didn't create the problem, wasn't my fault... let someone else deal with it." This is the kind of mentality that needs to be broken in Honduras because blaming others only fuels denial, laziness and apathy.

4. The fact that Honduras has re-established diplomatic relations with more than 50 countries is in no small part due to US efforts. If the US really wanted to punish and isolate Honduras for the long-term, it could easily have done so. Also, the word "interference" is subjective. If Honduras is willing to accept foreign aid, then it has to be willing to accept the conditions that come with that aid. Aid is almost always an investment, not a gift. That means that it comes with a price. That price can be interpreted as interference. It can also be interpreted as "looking out for an investment".

THE MARRIAGE OF HUGO CHÁVEZ AND MANUEL ZELAYA

March 9, 2010

It is unclear when the lovefest between Hugo Chávez and Manuel Zelaya actually began, although you can assume that it has been ongoing at least since their formal engagement on August 25, 2008 when Mr. Zelaya signed Honduras up for Mr. Chávez's ALBA alliance. The signing took place at the Presidential House in Tegucigalpa, complete with all the requisite pomp and circumstance and witnesses, including Evo Morales of Bolivia, Daniel Ortega of Nicaragua, Carlos Laje of Cuba, and even Roberto Micheletti. It has been a whirlwind engagement that began with Mr. Chávez showering Mr. Zelaya with all sorts of presents to demonstrate his affection.

While he was president of Honduras, Mr. Zelaya received gifts of cheap oil and untold amounts of cash from Mr. Chávez, who regularly called Mr. Zelaya on his cell phone to advise him, compliment him and build up his ego, and reassure him of his undying support and commitment. Mr. Chávez even sent Mr. Zelaya a planeload of ballots generously printed in Venezuela for him to use to gauge the Honduran public's interest in *la cuarta urna* referendum on rewriting the Constitution.

The Establishment in Honduras was uneasy with the engagement from the very start, but it was willing to give Mr. Zelaya the benefit of the doubt... for a while anyway. But as the months went by, it became evident that Mr. Zelaya was increasingly acting and sounding more like a protégé of Mr. Chávez than the person he was when he began his presidency in 2006. In one of his many long-winded speeches, Mr. Zelaya made reference to the concern that some people felt about his politics being of the "center-left". In a display of provocative *braggadocio*, Mr. Zelaya went on to suggest that they should just go ahead then and remove the word "center" and be done with it.

Mr. Chávez was seducing Mr. Zelaya and winning over his mind and soul, and to the Establishment it appeared as if there would be no turning back. He had gotten himself way too wrapped up with the smooth-talking wealthy guy from the south and was hopelessly smitten.

As so often happens in long-distance affairs of the heart that do not give sufficient consideration to the feelings of the couple's families and friends, they become messy and turbulent, and someone always ends up getting hurt. That is precisely what happened to Mr. Zelaya. His family disowned and banished him. They warned him repeatedly that this Chávez fellow was no good for him and brought nothing but trouble for the family. Mr. Zelaya would not listen. He would not give up the engagement. So he had to go.

For most of the initial three months following his banishment, Mr. Zelaya was taken care of by Mr. Chávez, who willingly provided a generous expense account and a private jet to whisk Mr. Zelaya and his friends up and down the Western Hemisphere to seek help in intervening with his family on his behalf. In return, Mr. Zelaya remained faithful to Mr. Chávez despite the fact that it was his relationship with him that got him shunned by his family and many of his friends.

If anything, Mr. Zelaya's banishment has drawn him even closer to Mr. Chávez... so much so, in fact, that during his surprise trip last week to visit Mr. Chávez at his house in

Caracas, the *Palacio Miraflores*, Mr. Zelaya was asked to tie the knot, and he accepted. At one hour past midnight on Friday, it was announced that Mr. Chávez and Mr. Zelaya were now officially joined. Mr. Zelaya would be Mr. Chávez's man in Petrocaribe, with perhaps one of the longest titles in the history of Latin American wordy titles... "Chief Political Consultant for Petrocaribe for the Process of Strengthening the Political Independence and Defense of Popular Democracy in Latin America and the Caribbean".

At the announcement in the Palace, Mr. Zelaya could hardly contain his emotions. He said that Mr. Chávez was his inspiration and the example that he sought to emulate. It was all so touching that it nearly made you want to forget about the incalculable pain, suffering, and chaos the affair has caused.

So now Mr. Chávez and Mr. Zelaya are one. The honeymoon has begun. The marriage may well succeed, or it may be short-lived once the two get to know each other more intimately. The engagement worked nicely. But long-distance relationships often tend to make the heart grow fonder. It's a little different when you start living together.

NOTES

Mr. Zelaya has often denied the extent of Mr. Chávez's influence on him. But by his own admission, Mr. Zelaya clearly states how much he was inspired by and admires Mr. Chávez. The consummation of the marriage between Mr. Zelaya and Mr. Chávez is good news for Honduras. Now, the two are officially linked. Seeing what is going on in Venezuela, it seems certain that Mr. Chávez does not have a bright future. When he falls, Mr. Zelaya will find himself in a huge dilemma... a man without a country, perhaps without much money, and probably without a cause, given that he may now be perceived as having sold out to Mr. Chávez. As Mr. Chávez's representative, Mr. Zelaya may increasingly identify less with his own supporters in Honduras. He will increasingly lose touch with his own original cause in Honduras. Talk about political suicide.

THE LAST GREAT HONDURAN COUP

March 9, 2010

Barack Obama is a socialist. I disagree with that opinion. Jesus of Nazareth should be worshipped more as a deity who created the universe than for the greatness of his humanity and wisdom. I do not share that sentiment. Sarah Palin is fit to be president of the United States. I have a real problem with that one. Look, reasonable people can disagree on countless issues, interpretations, and doctrines, particularly when it comes to politics and religion. The trick is not to let our differences consume us and lead us to do nasty things like discriminate, belittle, or get violent. One of the biggest disagreements related to Honduras has to do with whether or not the ousting of Manuel Zelaya was a "military coup". That squabble is probably destined to have a very long life-span.

While the removal of Mr. Zelaya may have been many things that could be argued to be illegal or wrong, it was clearly not a power grab by Honduras' military establishment. This realization was heightened a couple of days ago when General Romeo Vásquez, who recently retired as head of Honduras' Armed Forces, was appointed to manage Hondutel. That is a far cry from anything resembling a "power grab". General Vásquez was the man in charge of the military when Mr. Zelaya was arrested and flown to Costa Rica to commence his ordeal. From day one, General Vásquez said that he was acting under orders from the Supreme Court of Justice, led by Judge Jorge Alberto Rivera.

If what occurred in Honduras was a coup, then, if anything, it would be more accurately described as a "judicial coup". But somehow that wording does not carry near the same dramatic punch as a "military coup". Most people would not even know what to make of a judicial coup. But a military coup... that's something people can easily get their arms around.

The last "great" military coup that occurred in Honduras was not on June 28, 2009, but rather on October 3, 1963 when Colonel Osvaldo López Arellano overthrew the democratically elected President Ramón Villeda Morales in a bloody military coup that resulted in the deaths of hundreds of people and kept the Honduran military in power for the succeeding two decades. Ironically, it was the Liberal Party's nomination of Modesto Rodas Alvarado (against the wishes of fellow Liberal President Villeda) to run in the presidential election scheduled for October 13, 1963 that scared the military so much that some of its brass felt they had to act. Mr. Rodas, who was the father of former Foreign Minister and ideological mentor in the Zelaya administration, Patricia Rodas, was considered to be far too much of a political leftist at a time when there was an elevated fear of communism in Latin America. (Remember that Fidel Castro had come to power in Cuba in 1959.)

Throughout the 1960s and 1970s, Honduras was governed mostly by a successive series of military dictators. In his first stint as "president", López Arellano ruled until 1971 when he allowed for elections in April won by Ramón Cruz Uclés of the Nationalist Party. Mr. Cruz was installed as president on June 7, 1971. After serving only 18 months, President Cruz was removed from power on December 7, 1972 by General Oswaldo López Arelleno in another military coup. General López served as president until April 22, 1975 when he was ousted by another military coup orchestrated by his colleague, General Juan Melgar Castro.

General Melgar was overthrown in a bloodless coup in late-1978 by yet another general, Policarpo Paz García. It was General Paz who in 1980 decided to restore civil power in Honduras under a new constitution. The Honduran military did not give up the reins of power until January 27, 1982, when Roberto Suazo Córdova of the Liberal Party was inaugurated as Honduras' president. Mr. Suazo had been elected in November 1981.

If Mr. Zelaya's overthrow was a military coup, then it was one sorry example of one. On the one hand, you have Oswaldo López Arelleno who was obviously consumed by power and would not go away quietly. On the other, you have Romeo Vásquez, who is now the manager of a phone company.

NOTES

The Constitution favors the anti-*Zelayistas* in some Articles and tends to disfavor them in others. Reasonable people can have different opinions about Mr. Zelaya's overthrow. Even many of the Constitutional experts disagree with each other. Any document can be interpreted in many ways, depending on one's agenda. Individuals like Mr. Zelaya occasionally gain access to extreme power and refuse to let go. They force people to take drastic measures to get rid of them. It does not make the drastic measures right, but it may make them necessary.

MEL'S FEAR OF THE UNKNOWN

March 23, 2010

The news that President Lobo is willing to allow Manuel Zelaya to return to Honduras whenever he wishes should not surprise or shock anyone. Ever since the Honduran Congress passed an amnesty decree the day before Mr. Lobo's inauguration, it has been common knowledge that Mr. Zelaya would not be held accountable for political offenses he was alleged to have committed during his term in office. Mr. Lobo has wisely never expressed any interest in persecuting Mr. Zelaya, preferring instead to allow Mr. Zelaya to maintain some semblance of dignity for himself by giving him some space to maneuver so that he feels like he has reasonable options. It's called damage control. As much as many people in Honduras would like Mr. Lobo to persecute Mr. Zelaya and make him pay for the trauma he has inflicted upon the fabric of Honduran society, Mr. Lobo understands that Mr. Zelaya is toxic and thus better kept at arms length.

Mr. Lobo's willingness to allow Mr. Zelaya to travel to the Dominican Republic as a "Distinguished Guest" riled many Hondurans who felt that he was succumbing to coercion by the US State Department and that Mr. Zelaya was getting off the hook way too easily. Many feared that Mr. Zelaya should have been imprisoned so he could not be free to eternally cause trouble for Honduras. People said they wanted justice, but what many of them really wanted was revenge.

There are many good reasons for leaving Mr. Zelaya alone. The best one was given by Foreign Minister Mario Canahuati a couple of days ago when he said that the Honduran government simply does not have the time. I suspect he was also thinking "stomach". Given all of Honduras' economic and social problems, the country does not have the luxury of continuing to fuel the drama and the ego of one man who would like nothing better than to remain in the public limelight.

Mr. Lobo understands that the best way to deal with Mel Zelaya is to treat him nicely, respectfully, and gracefully... but to largely ignore him. The worst punishment for Mr. Zelaya is not persecution or imprisonment, which just serve to feed his image of himself as a martyr. The worst punishment for Mel is to be treated as inconsequential and irrelevant.

The truth is that Mr. Zelaya is old news. He is a man without a party, probably without a career, and someone who is no longer welcomed in polite society. He can no longer claim to be the legitimate president of Honduras because his term lapsed on January 27 and because all but a few nations have moved, or are in the process of moving, to recognize President Lobo. Honduras is slowly returning to normal, and that weakens Mr. Zelaya's hand.

Mr. Zelaya's only real base of organized support in Honduras is among *la Resistencia* which is now doing what all young activist movements do – bickering, pointing fingers, and breaking up into different factions. And even if *la Resistencia* were strong and united, Mr. Zelaya is not a true revolutionary; he only plays at it. If he were, he would already have taken Congress up on its amnesty gift and returned to Honduras to lead his supporters. Instead, Mr. Zelaya remains sequestered (yet again) in a luxury home in Santo Domingo, paid for either by the Dominican taxpayer or Hugo Chávez.

There is nothing preventing Mr. Zelaya from returning to Honduras except his own fears of the unknown. He knows that he can return and be greeted warmly as a hero by *la Reisistencia*. But while this is the part of Honduran society with which he most identifies politically, it is not the part of Honduran society with which he feels most comfortable associating on a daily basis.

Mr. Zelaya is part of the elite landowning class in Honduras. He is not accustomed to the difficult life. He fears that he will return to Honduras and be shunned by those whom he views as his cultural equals. Mr. Zelaya is part of the Establishment. He knows how to function within a system that respects his former title and his family name, wealth and connections – a system that gives people like him an automatic pass even when they are facing criminal charges. People like Mr. Zelaya are used to free passes in life, and the idea that he would have to go humbly before a judge and actually defend himself like a commoner is no doubt a scary and demeaning proposition.

Without being part of this system, Mr. Zelaya faces the challenge of having to go out among the people and work hard to strengthen and expand the movement that his ousting birthed. I don't think he relishes this kind of work because he is not an authentic revolutionary or even a competent community organizer. Creating a new society that is better than the existing one requires more creative ideas, grunt work, and vision than Mr. Zelaya has ever displayed. It is uncharted ground.

The news isn't that President Lobo is open to Mr. Zelaya's return. The news is why is it that Mr. Zelaya isn't jumping at the opportunity to return?

A Purgatorial Play for Pity

April 28, 2010

There are few things more pitiful to observe than a former leader of a country who craves desperately not to be forgotten after it is clear that his time has passed and the people who once supported him no longer place him at the forefront of their agenda and have, in fact, moved on to other matters that do not necessarily even require his presence. It is embarrassing to see a former leader attempt to shame his supporters for having cast him aside, and then proceed to wallow in martyrial self-pity by referring to all the sacrifices that he made for them and the suffering that he continues to endure in exile. It is sad to watch a former leader cling to the delusion that he remains relevant and wonder why he has disappeared from the newspapers, why he is no longer the topic of popular debate or the target of criticism by his political opponents... why he no longer is given the courtesy of having his existence acknowledged.

The surprise return of former First Lady Xiomara Zelaya to Honduras on Sunday is starting to provide some glimpses into the mental and emotional state of her husband, Manuel Zelaya, who remains in a kind of self-imposed purgatory in the Dominican Republic, mainly because he faces numerous criminal counts in Honduras to which he would have to answer were he to venture back. Mrs. Zelaya says that the conditions are not right for her husband to return to Honduras because there still exists an outstanding order for his arrest. Nonetheless, it appears that Mrs. Zelaya's visit is meant, at least in part, to relay a message from her husband to Hondurans, and specifically members of the National Resistance Front.

In a letter addressed to the National Resistance Front in Olancho, Mr. Zelaya writes:

"Friends, you know that I am suffering an unjust exile on the island that has given me asylum, the Dominican Republic – separated from a large portion of my family, my property and my country. I wish to take this opportunity to inform you that despite developing a great movement, the leaders of the National Resistance have left me out of their strategy, which should be focused on securing my return to my country to recover my rights as an Honduran. With such a strategy, which evidently forgets and fails to take me into consideration, they strengthen the plan by the *golpistas* to keep me away, isolated, and persecuted."

The letter continues...

"They minimize the possibility of my return when they gather signatures of support only for *la Constituyente*, forgetting who initiated the fight for *la Constituyente*, who is living in exile for the cause of *la Constituyente*, who gave all and lost all for the people, and is facing charges of treason and capture orders because I have called for the establishment of *la Constituyente*. I continue to hope for a prompt and wise resolution. My life remains at risk. I am constantly threatened. I am living here with part of my family, with few resources, including the light of solidarity from the international community. I am exiled for fighting for the poor and for justice."

and painfully continues...

"I ask myself what would motivate a president to risk everything, even his life, and to confront the powers that be and the enemies of democracy, offering and risking his family, wealth and even his life? What would move one to give everything and lose everything for the cause of democracy, coldy perhaps but with no bad intentions? I do not know. And after all this, his friends push him aside and leave him ostracized."

and mercifully concludes...

"Fellow countryman and friends, forgive my observations and proposals, but take them as the right of a good Honduran to express himself and who yearns to return to his country, to the land that gave birth to him in Olancho, and to be by the people's side in the fight for the independence and liberty of a country that will never abandon its children. Best wishes to my friends, to my mother in Olancho, and my companions in the Resistance. "Mel" Zelaya, April 25, 2010, the Dominican Republic."

❧

ZAPATERO'S PICKLE

May 5, 2010

Spain is in a predicament. No, not the fact that the country is on the verge of defaulting on its national debt, thus threatening to widen the already serious European debt crisis that has made the international headlines with mass riots in Greece. The government of Prime Minister José Luis Rodríguez Zapatero has been given a public ultimatum by leaders of the twelve-member Union of South American Nations (Unasur), including President Luiz Inácio Lula da Silva of Brazil, President Hugo Chávez of Venezuela, and President Rafael Correa of Ecuador. The fellas from down under have said that they will not attend the European Union-Latin America and Carribbean (EU-LAC) Summit hosted by Mr. Zapatero in Madrid on May 18 if President Porfirio Lobo shows up.

The problem for Mr. Zapatero is that his government has already extended an invitation to President Lobo to attend the summit, and Mr. Lobo has gladly accepted. The EU-LAC is a biennial meeting of the heads of state of Latin American, Caribbean, and EU countries. It is viewed as an important meeting for strengthening cooperation between the regions. The theme of the upcoming summit is, "Towards a new phase of the bi-regional association: innovation and technology for sustainable development and social inclusion".

Mr. Zapatero's invitation made sense, given that Spain has recognized the Lobo administration and re-established diplomatic ties with Honduras following a temporary break in relations after the overthrow of Manuel Zelaya as president last summer. Unfortunately for Mr. Zapatero, all but Colombia and Perú in Unasur have opted not to recognize President Lobo's government and have now issued an ultimatum to the Spanish prime minister: Either Pepe stays home, or we do.

It will be a huge embarrassment to Mr. Zapatero if Argentina, Bolivia, Brazil, Chile, Ecuador, Guyana, Paraguay, Suriname, Uruguay, and Venezuela do not send representatives to Madrid. Consequently, Mr. Zapatero is furiously working to patch together a compromise deal that would allow everyone to save their overly-sized Latin egos. Mr. Zapatero seems to think that all would be placated if the Lobo administration were to simply allow Mr. Zelaya to re-enter Honduras under some sort of special status that would absolve him, at least temporarily, of any responsibilities to appear before magistrates to answer to a long list of criminal charges against him.

Mr. Zapatero thinks this kind of "good faith gesture" just might do the trick. However, he is probably setting himself up for a rude awakening. While Mr. Lobo would be more than willing to personally greet Mr. Zelaya at Toncontín airport in Tegucigalpa and treat him with tremendous respect, the idea of interfering in Honduras' judicial process (as imperfect as that process may be) on behalf of such a controversial figure would be too politically dangerous at a time when Honduras is facing such an enormous list of social and economic problems.

Leaders such as Presidents Lula, Chávez, and Correa want to see Mr. Zelaya be permitted to play an active role in Honduran politics, unencumbered by pesky legal problems. But this will not happen, because Mr. Zelaya's time has passed, and those who insist on keeping this story alive have their own agendas that have nothing to do with the development and stability of Honduras.

Ultimately, Mr. Zapatero will have to make a choice. Either he accepts a much-reduced list of attendees for the meeting in Madrid, or he retracts his invitation to Mr. Lobo. It is hard to imagine a scenario where Mr. Zapatero would bow to the wishes of the South Americans. Spain is already looking extremely vulnerable from a financial standpoint. It cannot afford to appear politically weak by allowing itself to be coerced by a group of leaders under the influence of someone like Mr. Chávez.

MEL'S PERPLEXING PRISON PARANOIA

May 6, 2010

Manuel Zelaya's fear of being captured by Honduran security forces and imprisoned borders on the absurd, and it would be pathetic were it not so illogical. By now, it surely must have begun to sink in that the last thing the Lobo administration wants is to place Mr. Zelaya in a cell and have to take responsibility for this troublesome man. From the day Mr. Zelaya was overthrown as president, all anybody really wanted was to be rid of the guy. General Romeo Vásquez did not want to imprison Mel in Honduras, so he thoughtlessly shipped him off to Costa Rica. Interim president Roberto Micheletti did not want to imprison Mel, so he let him hang out as long as he wished at the Brazilian embassy. President Lobo did not want to imprison Mel, so he escorted him to the airport and gladly allowed him fly off to the Dominican Republic under the status of "Distinguished Guest". What is it about this picture that Mr. Zelaya cannot seem to comprehend?

While there is an outstanding capture order for Mr. Zelaya that was issued by Honduras' Public Ministry and Attorney General for alleged crimes committed during his administration – including misappropriation of public funds, theft, and corruption – it is clear that no one is interested in taking the man into custody and creating another circus. The Lobo administration has neither the stomach nor the budget for it. President Lobo, in fact, confirmed yesterday that Mr. Zelaya would not be arrested were he to return to Honduras. He said that he was reassured of this by the Supreme Court. "The Court has told me... we understand the law and the need for justice to be served, but we also understand the reality of the political situation that we face as Hondurans."

Honduras' Minister of Security Óscar Álvarez has said that he would be obligated by law to arrest Mr. Zelaya were he to re-enter Honduras. But that is what he has to say... officially. There has been a capture order out for the former director of the National Telecommunications Commission (Conatel) and chief Zelaya aide, Rasel Tomé. He returned in March. He has neither been jailed nor bothered very much. The same is true for former Vice-President Arístides Mejía, former Minister of Finance Rebeca Santos, and the former manager of the National Electrical Power Company (Enee), Rixi Moncada.

What Mr. Zelaya fails to consider is that it would represent a lot of work and an endless series of headaches for the Lobo administration to keep behind bars a former president who was overthrown in what at least most of the world believes was a coup. Probably the worst that could happen to Mr. Zelaya is that he would be summoned to appear before a magistrate in Tegucigalpa to be formally presented with the criminal charges against him. The judge, Mr. Zelaya, and the attorneys present would be served coffee and cookies. They would then proceed to have a nice, informal chat. Mr. Zelaya would be asked not to leave the country without first notifying the court. He'd say, "Of course, no problem." He would go home and not be troubled again by any official of note unless he decided to do something silly like incite a riot.

Either Mr. Zelaya has such an extreme phobia of imprison-ment that it prohibits him from contemplating even a minute risk of this possibility or he has so much pride that he cannot bear the scenario of humbling himself before a judge. Elements of both may be in play. More than likely, though,

Mr. Zelaya is simply continuing to play politics and milking the role of martyr for all it's worth. So long as he can claim that he is being persecuted by the Lobo administration, Mr. Zelaya can remain in the newspaper headlines and delude himself into believing that he remains relevant in Honduras.

It must be abhorrent for someone like Mr. Zelaya to think that he is not even worthy of being captured and imprisoned. It would mean that he might finally have to accept that his time has passed, and that there is nothing left for him to do but quietly return to his ranch in Olancho.

EAGERLY AWAITING MEL'S MANIFESTO

May 12, 2010

It is customary for political theorists and leaders who want to change society to commit to paper their ideas and vision, so that others can understand their thought processes, their justifications, and their blueprints for implementation. Rousseau's 1762 treatise, *The Social Contract*, is said to have inspired the French Revolution. Thomas Paine's pamphlet *Common Sense*, written in 1776, made the case for the American Revolution. Marx and Engels wrote *The Communist Manifesto* in 1847. Lenin wrote *The State and Revolution* when he was hiding from persecution from the Provisional Government in Russia in 1917. Hitler wrote *Mein Kampf* when he was imprisoned for political crimes in 1923. As a prelude to his run for the presidency, Barack Obama wrote *The Audacity of Hope* in 2006. Even Ron Paul has a manifesto out called *The Revolution*.

In early March, Manuel Zelaya (who remains in comfortable exile in the Dominican Republic) said that he was planning to write a book about his overthrow. He said that he already had the concept in mind: "Petroleum and Coup d'État". He said he would complete the book within three months, which would roughly coincide with the infamous (or joyous, depending on your point of view) date of June 28. I look forward to reading the book, although I have my doubts it will ever be written, unless Mr. Zelaya decides to go ahead and contract a ghostwriter who would have the sufficient mental endurance to sit patiently and feign interest while the former president rambles aimlessly about his favorite subject... himself.

Mr. Zelaya's strong suit has never been a knack or fondness for writing, which explains why it is difficult to find copies of any articles or essays he has written during his lifetime, much less any books. About the most one is able to muster are a few odd letters and speeches, which contain no more than vague and generic propaganda or pleas for help or pity. The scarcity of penned works by Mr. Zelaya leads one to conclude that the man is more fluff than substance – an intellectual lightweight. Usually, when a leader is engaged in a history-making campaign to build a social movement and radically alter the status quo in a country, that individual sits down and writes what is on his or her mind, especially if that person happens to be in exile or in prison where there is ample time.

Serious leaders who seek to transform societies base their motivation on a clear set of concerns about the injustices and inequities that are present. They are guided by strong principles of what is right and wrong. They give a tremendous amount of thought to where they want to take the country and a clear vision of how they intend to get there. Mr. Zelaya has shown little propensity for clarity of concerns, principles or thought, which explains why he has not written anything of any consequence. It is amazing that none of Mr. Zelaya's followers or opponents have called him to task on this glaring gap.

Mr. Zelaya wants to establish a National Constituent Assembly to review and rewrite the Constitution. He wants to change Honduras from a representative democracy to a participatory democracy. He wants to shift the balance of power in the country from the "elite" to "the people". In short, he wants to start over and re-found Honduras. Yet Mr. Zelaya offers no detailed plan of action for how he intends to create his utopia without fueling mass chaos or possibly civil war. No treatise. No manifesto. No white paper. Not even so much as a policy brief.

Mr. Zelaya's supporters deserve more than a bland diet of canned speeches and clichés, more than empty promises from an individual who is little more than an amateurish dreamer who has brilliantly proven he cannot govern Honduras, much less transform Honduran society. Write your book Mr. Zelaya. Prove us wrong.

RETURN OF THE DOG-AND-PONY SHOW

May 14, 2010

Manuel Zelaya's surprise arrival in Nicaragua yesterday may be a sign that the former president has had all the rest and relaxation he needs in the Dominican Republic and is now feeling sufficiently re-energized to take his circus on the road again. From the day he was overthrown on June 28, 2009 and flown to Costa Rica until the day he snuck back into Honduras on September 21 and took up residence in the Brazilian embassy in Tegucigalpa, Mr. Zelaya toured up and down the Western Hemisphere aboard a private business jet, courtesy of Venezuela's President Hugo Chávez. His home base was Nicaragua's capital, Managua, and his host was that country's president, Daniel Ortega. After four months of refuge at the embassy and three and half months of self-imposed exile in the plush "Las Sierritas" neighborhood of the Dominican capital of Santo Domingo, Mr. Zelaya has come full circle.

It is almost as if Mr. Zelaya is pretending that the past seven and a half months never occurred. He is once again reunited with Mr. Ortega. He is reunited with his former Minister of Foreign Affairs, Patricia Rodas, who has been living in Nicaragua's second largest city, León. His wife, Xiomara, is back in Honduras, allowing Mr. Zelaya some freedom of mobility. And he has once again taken up the habit of aggressively making demands from afar from a position of weakness.

Much has happened since Mr. Zelaya was last in Nicaragua. For starters, Honduras elected a new president who has been recognized by the United States. Hmm, well... that's about all that really needs to be said. Thus, Mr. Zelaya will find relatively few governments in North or Central America that will be as receptive to him as they were last summer. He will certainly not be greeted warmly in Washington, DC or in Ottawa, and probably not in Mexico City either.

Given that the governments of Costa Rica, El Salvador, Guatemala, and Panama have all established close relations with the Lobo administration, Mr. Zelaya will not find ready forums in those countries where he can criticize and issue ultimatums to President Lobo. This time around, Mr. Zelaya's movements will largely be confined to Nicaragua and an occasional jaunt to South America. Nonetheless, the man can still pose a problem for Mr. Lobo. Perhaps the biggest danger is that Mr. Zelaya will be so consistently annoying that Mr. Lobo will falter and make the grave mistake of engaging in a public tit-for-tat with him. This would give Mr. Zelaya precisely what he craves... attention, and what he needs... traction. It would also distract Mr. Lobo from his focus on governing Honduras.

Mr. Lobo has been supremely patient and magnanimous toward Mr. Zelaya. He pushed for Congress to grant Mr. Zelaya amnesty for political offenses which included acts of sedition and terrorism, inciting public insurrection, vandalism, conspiring to distribute arms, and abuse of power. He avoided a confrontation with Mr. Zelaya by opting not to arrest him at the Brazilian embassy. Instead, he allowed Mr. Zelaya to save face by traveling to the Dominican Republic under the status of "Distinguished Guest", and has gone out of his way to avoid making remarks that could be interpreted as disparaging Mr. Zelaya in any way during his exile. On the contrary, Mr. Lobo has repeatedly said that Mr. Zelaya would be welcomed in

Honduras and treated with the respect owed to a former president.

Mr. Lobo's conciliatory tone toward Mr. Zelaya has come at a price. Many within Honduras have come to view Mr. Lobo as weak for the way in which he has dealt with Mr. Zelaya. They are now pointing to Mr. Zelaya's renewed troublemaking, and saying, "See, we told so... you should have put him away while you had the chance."

Mr. Lobo's approach toward Mr. Zelaya has been clever, wise, and sound. It has given Honduras time to begin healing and moving forward by not having to deal with daily doses of news about Mr. Zelaya. It has also prevented Mr. Zelaya from being transformed into something larger than what he is: an average guy with an unhealthy ego. Still, Mr. Lobo cannot completely ignore Mr. Zelaya, particularly now that he has re-surfaced for air next door in Nicaragua.

While he should refrain from making public statements about Mr. Zelaya, Mr. Lobo has to take Mr. Zelaya's public statements made in Nicaragua seriously. So long as Mr. Zelaya was holding tight in the Dominican Republic, he could do little to stir up trouble in Honduras. His presence in Nicaragua changes things. Further, Mr. Lobo may wish to re-evaluate his thinking about the courtesies Mr. Zelaya is due. While it is true that Mr. Zelaya is a former president, that position has since been eclipsed by Mr. Zelaya's role as an official operative of Mr. Chávez. On March 5, Mr. Chávez announced that Mr. Zelaya would join Venezuela's oil cooperative, Petrocaribe, appointing him "Chief Political Consultant for Petrocaribe for the Process of Strengthening the Political Independence and Defense of Popular Democracy in Latin America and the Caribbean".

In response, Mr. Zelaya credited Mr. Chávez for helping to initiate the process of change in Honduras. "You inspired us" said Mr. Zelaya emotionally. "You have resisted for ten years and you keep growing stronger. Changes do not come easy, it is hard work, but you are an example that it can be done; you inspire the revolution that we have begun in Honduras." He emphasized that his cause "is not lost".

In short, Mr. Zelaya is employed by a foreign government that does not recognize the current government of Honduras and whose leader is doing all he can to undermine it. He works for Mr. Chávez and is indebted to him financially and ideologically. There should be no question in Mr. Lobo's mind as to where Mr. Zelaya's sympathies and loyalties lie.

A CAMPAIGN OF CYNICAL IGNORANCE

May 20, 2010

There appears to be a sort of conspiracy of ignorance (or worse) by many international human rights organizations and many within the liberal media to paint Honduras as a hotbed of human rights violations linked to the "coup d'état" of President Manuel Zelaya last year. These groups are doing their utmost to avoid directly accusing the Lobo government of being responsible for a campaign of targeted assassinations and intimidation, while at the same time making public statements that imply precisely that. In a few cases, the accusations are far from veiled. Take, for example, a recent article by *Washington Post* writer Kari Lydersen titled, "Welcome To The New Honduras, Where Right-Wing Death Squads Proliferate".

Take also yesterday's remarks by Felipe González of the Inter-American Commission for Human Rights (IACHR) suggesting that the Lobo administration is doing nothing to investigate the human rights violations in Honduras, notably the murders of seven journalists since March 1. The message that Mr. González wishes to convey is that the government of Honduras is either behind the killings or opting to look the other way for some nefarious reason. The message is that there is a plot underway in Honduras by the country's governing elite to get back at anyone who opposed and continues to oppose the decision to remove Mr. Zelaya from power.

The problem with overly cynical conspiracy theories is that they award the governing infrastructure of Honduras way too much credit. It takes a lot to organize and sustain conspiracies. Sadly, Honduras just doesn't have what it takes. You see, the biggest problem in Honduras has never been that its leaders have been too corrupt, violent, or evil. The biggest problem has always been that they are incompetent, which explains why Honduras has always ranked as one of the three or four poorest countries in the Western Hemisphere. It is the poor leadership and the poverty that creates the fertile ground in which the violence and the killings can breed, thrive, and continue unabated.

The irony is that there has never been anyone in the history of Honduras who has better symbolized inept rule than Mr. Zelaya. Thus, a good deal of the violence and killings that human rights organizations and the liberal media have attributed to those who got rid of Mr. Zelaya and now govern Honduras is actually a result of Mr. Zelaya's horrid style of leadership.

The truth is that there is no grand conspiracy in Honduras. The violence and killings are primarily due to crime being allowed to run rampant. And this is not because President Lobo lacks the desire, will, or courage to respond, but rather because he has neither the financial resources, sufficient staffing and equipment, nor a brilliant enough strategy to combat these ominous threats to Honduran society.

By painting the Lobo government with broad negative strokes, human rights organizations and the media are actually hindering its ability to deal effectively with organized crime, out-of-control gangs, and the flood of illegal drugs into Honduras. It is not only damaging and unfair, it is misinformed and ignorant.

Other than the obvious fact that most of the homicides have been occurring in the areas of San Pedro Sula and Tegucigalpa, there are no discernable patterns. The killings are brutal, but they are mostly random. It's crime, not conspiracy. It is what happens in extremely poor countries with weak institutions of government and an apathetic wealthy and educated class of citizens who live in constant fear of their less fortunate and desperate neighbors.

NOTES

1. A major challenge for the Truth Commission will be to determine the circumstances of the alleged abuses. It is not enough to identify the abusers and the abused, it is also important to provide some perspective and context as to how confrontations developed – whether or not there were provocations, and if so, whether they were met with excessive and unreasonable force, and what defines "excessive" and "unreasonable".

2. The death of 29-year old Vanessa Zepeda on February 3 is an example of the difficulty that the Truth Commission will have in determining responsibility for the deaths of people in Honduras alleged to have been killed by the government. Mrs. Zepeda, a nurse at the Honduran Social Security Institute, left her home in Tegucigalpa at 2 pm. At about 6:30 pm, her body was dumped out of a vehicle in the Loarque neighborhood. Mrs. Zepeda was a SITRAIHASS union leader, and she had reportedly received numerous threats for her activities within the Resistance. The threats had been registered with various Honduran human rights organizations prior to Mrs. Zepeda's death. Does this case fall under the category of crime or political assassination?

A Tea Party for Honduras

President Porfirio Lobo today stated that he would willingly offer his support to members of the National Resistance Front Against the Coup d'État if they wished to incorporate as a political party in Honduras. The proposal is one of the conditions set forth by leaders of countries such as Brazil, Eduador, and Venezuela for recognition of the Lobo government. If you are thinking one-dimensionally and allowing your thoughts to be dominated by vague concepts of honor and pride, your initial reaction to President Lobo's position might be, "What?... is the man crazy?" But if you are thinking practically and strategically, you may begin to see the brilliance of this move, at least from the standpoint of the incumbent Nationalist Party.

From a practical standpoint, it makes sense to welcome *la Resistencia* into the official fold. It is less disturbing and destabilizing to the social and economic climate in the country to push *la Resistencia* more into the political mainstream, albeit on the far left. The important thing is to minimize the opportunities for angry people to amass in the streets in large numbers. The sooner members of *la Resistencia* stop feeling like outsiders, the sooner they will feel invested in the process of electoral politics and begin to reject the value of promoting revolution.

Recognition of your opponent may just feel plain wrong and dangerous. But think of it more as "co-opting", holding your opponent close where you can keep an eye on him, rather than allowing your opponent to go underground where you can't.

From a strategic standpoint, Mr. Lobo's offer to help *la Resistencia* become an official player in Honduran politics can be seen as a move to ensure the dominance of the Nationalist Party in national and local elections for the foreseeable future. The Liberal Party would be well advised to strongly oppose Mr. Lobo on this one. By enabling the creation of the "Resistance Party", Mr. Lobo would help solidify the severe divisions that already exist within the Liberal Party in Honduras – divisions that were apparent in his trouncing of Liberal presidential candidate Elvin Santos in the election of November 29.

Think what President Obama would do if he were asked to support the establishment of the "Tea Party" as an official political party in the United States. It's hard to imagine he would be anything less than an enthusiastic supporter of the idea. Republicans... not so much.

NOTES

No one knows exactly what is going on behind the scenes, but it is entirely possible that some members of the Liberal Party may have asked Ambassador Llorens to host a meeting to bring together different factions of the party out of concern that the party may quickly be on its way to becoming politically uncompetitive with the Nationalists because of the deep divisions that exist between anti- and pro-*Zelayistas*. Without a united Liberal Party, Honduras starts to transform into a country with one major party, which obviously reduces its credibility as a democracy. Unless there is true reconciliation within the Liberal Party, it is possible that the party will not win another presidential election for decades. Like it or not, Mr. Zelaya remains a factor in Honduran politics.

MEL'S PLAN FOR NATIONAL RECONCILIATION

May 28, 2010

Manuel Zelaya has been on the road during the past two weeks trying to sell a plan for national reconciliation in Honduras that he has devised. First, he went to visit President Rafael Correa in Ecuador. Then, he traveled to Nicaragua to spend a day with President Daniel Ortega before heading off to Cuba to meet with President Raúl Castro. It was in Nicaragua on May 13 that Mr. Zelaya first announced his plan, although he revealed few details about it.

As important as a "Plan for National Reconciliation" sounds, you would think that Mr. Zelaya would have written it down somewhere so that it could be seriously evaluated. You would think that one of his aides or advisors would have taken the initiative to commit their boss's ideas to paper. Nope. So let's give it a try here...

Based on Mr. Zelaya's public comments, it seems that his plan consists of one central point and three attached conditions. The central point is that those nations in Latin America and the Caribbean that have yet to recognize the Lobo government and re-establish full diplomatic relations with Honduras would grant this recognition and, further, support Honduras' readmission to regional organizations such as the Organization of American States (OAS) and the Central American Integration System (SICA) on the condition that:

1. President Lobo issue a declaration of amnesty to Mr. Zelaya for all of the criminal charges against him and allow Mr. Zelaya to return to Honduras without the threat of arrest or persecution.

2. President Lobo allow the National Resistance Front Against the Coup d'État to officially organize as a political party in Honduras, with all the requisite rights and privileges.

3. President Lobo permit Mr. Zelaya to participate freely in political activities in Honduras.

That's pretty much the extent of it.

The underlying assumption of the plan is that Mr. Zelaya's safe return to Honduras and the elimination of any efforts to hold him responsible for alleged crimes would signal the good faith required to begin healing the wounds left within Honduran society as a result of Mr. Zelaya's overthrow.

The recognition of *la Resistencia* as a political party would supposedly give legitimacy to the movement and facilitate its institutionalization so that it can more easily organize and grow, and thereby ensure its long-term survival.

Permitting Mr. Zelaya to engage in politics as he wishes would essentially leave him unrestrained either to try and regain a leadership role within the Liberal Party (as unlikely as that may be) or within the new far-left FNRP Party – *Frente Nacional de Resistencia Popular*. It would also make it easier for Mr. Zelaya to promote the political careers of his wife, Xiomara, and eventually his daughter, Xiomara Hortensia... thereby maintaining some hope of restoring the honor of the family name and even piecing together a political dynasty under his patronage.

Mr. Zelaya's plan may seem outrageous and dangerous, given how much division, hate, and fear this man has created in Honduras. Common sense would dictate that the longer Mr.

Zelaya stays away from Honduras, the better. But while the plan has nothing to do with national reconciliation and everything to do with Mel Zelaya, the truth is that a reasonable case can be made for granting two out of the three conditions.

The one condition that cannot be met is the first one. While President Lobo can guarantee that Mr. Zelaya will not be arrested and bothered too much by his administration, he cannot automatically pardon him for alleged crimes. Mr. Zelaya must at least go through the process of answering to the charges against him. He must act like an adult citizen, rather than a spoiled child.

⚜

Sowing Seeds of Suspicion

June 9, 2010

You have to wonder about the thoughts that must be running through Hugo Chávez's mind right now as he stares at the photograph of US Secretary of State Hillary Clinton warmly embracing President Rafael Correa of Ecuador. It must drive Mr. Chávez crazy wondering, "Why won't they fight fair!" Instead of engaging in a *machista*-style, insult-laden tit-for-tat with Mr. Chávez, the Obama administration continues its calm diplomacy with governments such as President Correa's that have not been particularly helpful to the United States in dealing with the political crisis in Honduras. On the issue of Manuel Zelaya, Mr. Correa has sought to thwart US diplomatic efforts every step of the way.

It has been less than a month since Mr. Zelaya was warmly greeted by Mr. Correa in Quito. Mr. Correa has been one of Mr. Zelaya's staunchest supporters and has been critical of the US government's apparent policy reversal toward Honduras after initially condemning Mr. Zelaya's overthrow last summer. Since the election of President Lobo, the US has worked closely with him to normalize bilateral relations, as well as Honduras' relations with other countries. The US has pretty much decided that Mr. Zelaya will have to fend for himself from now on.

Mr. Correa continues to be among those in Latin America who strongly oppose the readmission of Honduras into the

OAS unless Mr. Zelaya is welcomed back to Honduras as some sort of national hero. The Obama administration, on the other hand, has been actively pushing for Honduras' immediate reincorporation into the inter-American system, arguing that the Lobo administration has been more than responsive to conditions set forth by the international community to demonstrate Honduras' return to constitutional government.

Mrs. Clinton's visit with Mr. Correa is mostly a goodwill trip designed to smooth over some of the difficulties between the US and Ecuador, particularly with regard to US military bases in neighboring Colombia. It is also meant to look for ways in which the two countries can cooperate more on combating illegal drug trafficking. Don't be surprised if Mrs. Clinton puts in a good word for Honduras as well and manages to soften Ecuador's position with regard to the Lobo government.

The overarching goal of Mrs. Clinton's visit may well be to continue to find weak spots in the relationships between certain South American countries and Venezuela. The idea is to slowly drive a wedge – rock the boat a bit – between friends like Mr. Correa and Mr. Chávez by providing gentle reminders that Mr. Chávez is ultimately a losing proposition and that there is much more to be gained from expanded ties with the US. If nothing else, a little hand-holding and a few photo ops between Mrs. Cinton and Mr. Correa may plant just enough of a seed of suspicion in Mr. Chávez's head to begin to stir up trouble within the ALBA bloc in South America that Mr. Chávez has invested so much of his time and money piecing together.

NOTES

1. Much has been made about the Obama administration's

condemnation of the ousting of Mr. Zelaya. Many could not understand what good reason the US could have for at least appearing to support Mr. Zelaya. There are many good reasons, but one of the best has to do with building a case for the readmission of Honduras into the inter-American system. Had the US treated Mr. Zelaya disrespectfully, fully backed the Micheletti government and not brokered the Tegucigalpa-San José Accord (calling for the Truth and Reconciliation Commission), which ultimately led to the peaceful election of Porfirio Lobo, Secretary of State Clinton would lack a credible case to make on behalf of Honduras at the OAS meeting in Lima today. It is not difficult to see that Honduras would have remained isolated in the world for years absent a good case for why it should be accepted once again.

2. Given the tainted history of US involvement in Latin America during the past century, US credibility when it comes to anything that even vaguely has the air of a coup is zilch. This was an extremely well played match by the US from the start, and now we are getting yet another glimpse as to why it had to be played the way it was. The US is now able to be a credible advocate for Honduras' readmission to the OAS. Had it clearly sided with the Micheletti government, the US would be a non-player, which means that Mr. Chávez, Mr. Lula and all the other Unasur leaders would have much stronger positions.

MORE COCA FOR EVO

June 25, 2010

Ecuador's Foreign Minister, Ricardo Patiño, added a touch of drama yesterday to the opening ceremony of the ALBA Summit in Quito, Ecuador when he said that the "spirit of Honduras" was present at the gathering even though the country officially withdrew its membership in the alliance on January 27, 2010 and was thus absent. Former president Manuel Zelaya signed Honduras up for ALBA on August 25, 2008, but the relationship quickly soured following Mr. Zelaya's overthrow on June 28, 2009. Today, Bolivia's president, Evo Morales, seemed to be taking his cue from Mr. Patiño when he assigned responsibility to the "dictatorship" in Honduras for the Honduran national soccer team's failure to advance to the second round of the World Cup. It was a low blow even for Mr. Morales, who has a reputation for saying silly things in public.

You have to wonder what fuels the brain cells of Mr. Morales for him to even associate the performance of a soccer team with certain political players and events. Clearly, Mr. Morales feels the need to attack the Lobo administration and anyone who remotely supported the removal of Mr. Zelaya, directly or indirectly. It is not enough to continue engaging in the wholly uncreative and unproductive exercise of name-calling and to stubbornly refuse to recognize the Lobo government. Now, Mr. Morales (no doubt egged on by his ALBA associates) figures, "Why not blame those horrid

golpistas for their team's poor showing at the World Cup?"
Yep, that's bound to hurt, annoy, and discredit them.

There are four problems with Mr. Morales' thinking. The
first is that it is infantile. It sounds like a bully lobbing insult
after insult in the hope that one will eventually hit its mark and
sting. The second is that it is based on the inaccurate
assumption that Honduras' inability to reach the "Sweet
Sixteen" in the World Cup is a failure. The reality is that for a
small and impoverished country like Honduras to even qualify
for the World Cup is a major accomplishment that makes any
characterization of its team's participation as anything less
than successful sound absurd. In other words, Honduras was a
winner even before it took the field in its opening match
against Chile on June 16.

Mr. Morales' third problem is that in the process of
blaming the Lobo government for the "failure" of Honduras at
the World Cup, Evo pretty much insulted the Honduran
national team. In most countries where soccer is the national
pastime and perhaps the greatest source of national pride, the
last thing you want to do is belittle the national team. It is akin
to insulting the country. So my guess is that Mr. Morales
might just have cleverly earned himself the ire of most
Hondurans, including those who may have once sympathized
with him. The same thing happened when President Arias of
Costa Rica referred to the Honduran Constitution as the "worst
in the world". People tend not to forget or forgive these kind of
disparaging remarks.

Oh yes... the fourth problem with Mr. Morales' thinking.
While it is true that Honduras did not perform well enough to
make it to the second round of the World Cup, it is also
painfully true that Bolivia did not even qualify to participate in
the tournament. No invitations to the show. No plane tickets.
No photo ops. No memories. Zilch... *nada.* Mr. Morales must
logically accept full blame for this failure. Somehow, he jinxed

his team, or he did something that caused it to fall short of expectations.

While the Honduran team has been in South Africa playing its heart out and making history before stadium crowds of tens of thousands of people and television, radio, and Internet audiences of tens of millions around the world, taking on strong and well-funded teams from Chile, Spain, and Switzerland, and playing them close, the Bolivian team has... well, been sitting at home... watching Honduras on TV. Same as the other seven ALBA teams.

Former Presidents Need Benefits

June 27, 2010

Practically no one believes that former president Manuel Zelaya, who remains in self-exile in the Dominican Republic, would be denied his human or civil rights were he to return to Honduras. Few people truly believe that he would be flogged and then tossed into a prison cell by the Lobo government were he to simply choose to board a commercial aircraft and fly to Tegucigalpa like his chief aide, Rasel Tomé, did on March 11 and his wife, Xiomara, did on April 25. Hardly anyone seriously believes Mr. Zelaya would be denied the same genteel and fair treatment accorded to his former top Ministers – Arístides Mejía, Rixi Moncada, and Rebeca Santos who have all been charged with criminal acts and asked to submit their testimonies to Honduran magistrates, which they have done without incident.

I suspect that not even Mr. Zelaya honestly believes that he would be treated badly or persecuted by the Lobo government. Mr. Zelaya is a person with too high an international profile now for President Lobo to treat with anything other than kid gloves and even a little deference. The Lobo government has everything to lose and nothing to gain by handling Mr. Zelaya roughly. It is already widely perceived around the world that Mr. Zelaya was given the short end of the stick and has suffered unjustly. President Lobo cannot afford to be portrayed as someone who would further shame a defeated opponent while down.

By offering several times to travel to the Dominican Republic to escort Mr. Zelaya back to Honduras, President Lobo has put out the message, "Look, I'll even take personal responsibility for the man's safe return." A gutsy move, albeit a clumsy one. President Lobo has also publicly reassured Mr. Zelaya that he has spoken with Honduras' Public Ministry and Attorney General (those who have issued arrest orders for Mr. Zelaya for numerous criminal counts), and that they promised he would not be arrested. All Mr. Zelaya would be required to do is present himself before the courts to answer to the charges.

Mr. Zelaya has stated that he wants full immunity from all criminal charges. President Lobo has told him that amnesty is out of the question because that would blatantly undermine Honduras' judicial system. Congress (with President Lobo's blessing) has already granted Mr. Zelaya amnesty for a series of political offenses related to his efforts to promote and hold an opinion poll and *la cuarta urna* referendum to change the Constitution. For alleged criminal actions, Mr. Zelaya would have to prove his innocence like any responsible citizen. Otherwise, it would only confirm the widely held view that some political leaders are above the law.

Mr. Zelaya's demand for amnesty is no more than a ruse, perhaps intended to hide the real reason he is so reluctant to return to his homeland. It has nothing to do with him being persecuted or imprisoned by the Lobo government. It has everything to do with the Lobo government not being willing to protect Mr. Zelaya and provide him all the amenities and privileges – including a life-time salary, a seat in the Central American Parliament (Parlacen), free entry into special events, and a full-time security detail – normally given to a former head of state. In other words, were Mr. Zelaya to venture back into Honduras, he would be on his own.

Without all of these fringe benefits, a former president like Mr. Zelaya, who angered a lot of people and no doubt made more than a few enemies, would be left uncomfortably exposed. Remember, Mr. Zelaya is not a rich man like some of his predecessors. Ironically, he needs to rely on the government (which he continues to antagonize) for his own protection. When Mr. Zelaya demands that the Lobo government protect him, he means exactly that. It is not that he fears the government, rather he fears the government will ignore him.

The Good Leadership Gap

June 28, 2010

Responding to cynical comments delivered at the Republican National Convention mocking then-Senator Barack Obama's experience as a community organizer, campaign manager David Plouffe said, "Community organizing is how ordinary people respond to out-of-touch politicians and their failed policies." He added, "Throughout our history, ordinary people have made good on America's promise by organizing for change from the bottom up." This perspective on leadership gets to the heart of why so many issues and problems in societies go unaddressed and unresolved.

The idea that change is a process that should start from the top and filter down to the bottom is certainly prevalent in Honduras, and this – perhaps more than anything else – is the reason that the social and economic situation in the country never seems to get any better for the vast majority of Hondurans. Most are awaiting solutions and vision from those who hold official positions within institutions such as the government and the Church when there are so many other individuals in communities throughout Honduras who possess the kind of ideas, energy, and resolve to truly transform the country, but they either do not know it or are not finding (or being allowed) the opportunities to lead.

One of the problems is that the traditional image of leaders is extremely narrow, confined to those relatively few "above" us

236

rather than encompassing many of those around us as well. The fact is that the wisest, most intelligent, and most capable of us are not necessarily the ones who have been elected or appointed to an office. And all too often those who have been elected or appointed to lead within institutions grow more interested in protecting their positions than serving the interests of the people for whom the institutions were created to serve in the first place. The tendency then is to try and preserve the status quo rather than effectively deal with difficult issues and problems. Nothing gets done, and thus things continue to fall apart.

So the question is, "Who are the truly great leaders of Honduras today, and where should we look for them in the future?" Perhaps more to the point, though, "What key traits must be present in someone for that person to be the kind of leader that Honduras needs in order to escape its cycles of bad times and less bad times?" One clue: our traditional conceptions of and qualifications for leadership have not served Honduras well.

The End of Liberalism in Honduras?

July 19, 2010

The willingness of President Porfirio Lobo to support the process to officially recognize the National Front for Popular Resistance (FNRP) – *la Resistencia* – as a political party in Honduras is seen by some as sheer lunacy. They wonder why President Lobo would wish to give legitimacy to a far-left movement like the FNRP, particularly when there is a widely held perception in Honduras that it is a violent and destabilizing force in the country. Some people speculate that Mr. Lobo must secretly sympathize with the FNRP or is being forced by the US government to accept the organization. But such reasoning is irrational.

From Mr. Lobo's standpoint, there are two primary reasons for welcoming the FNRP into mainstream party politics in Honduras. Neither of them has anything to do with sympathy for the organization and its limited and vague agenda. The first reason is simply that it is preferable to have a radical and angry social movement openly play your game according to a set of rules with which you are familiar and comfortable rather than risk it becoming so radicalized that it evolves into an armed and violent movement that goes underground and becomes uncontrollable.

The appearance of lending legitimacy to the FNRP is a small price to pay, compared to the potential price of ignoring the organization and pretending it will eventually disappear.

The truth is that most of the concerns and demands of the FNRP are legitimate. What may be questionable are the group's day-to-day tactics and overall long-term strategy, which includes setting up a National Constituent Assembly to rewrite the Constitution.

The second reason Mr. Lobo views bringing the FNRP into the mainstream political fold as a good thing is that it automatically strengthens the position of his Nationalist Party. The Nationalist Party has always been smaller than the Liberal Party in Honduras, which is partly why it has traditionally had a harder time winning the presidency. One of its advantages is that it tends to be a more unified party than the Liberals, and its base of support comes from the wealthy business class. When the Liberal Party experiences divisions within its ranks or is unable to fully mobilize its base, which is largely the poor and lower middle classes, then the Nationalists tend to do much better in national elections.

When Honduras returned to democratic rule in 1982, following two decades of military dictatorships, it did so under a Liberal president, Roberto Suazo. President Suazo was followed in 1986 by another Liberal, José Azcona. In 1990, the Nationalists won the presidency with Rafael Callejas and then lost it again in 1994 to the Liberal Party's Carlos Reina and yet again in 1998 to the Liberal's Carlos Flores. A Nationalist, Ricardo Maduro, finally returned to the presidency in 2002. In 2006, it was again another Liberal, Manuel Zelaya.

The Liberal Party wins the presidency two out of every three elections, and so there is always more of a sense of urgency within the Nationalist Party to look for ways to gain an edge whenever and wherever it can. This "edge" may now very well be that segment of the Liberal electorate that is unhappy with and, in fact, hostile toward the Liberal Party.

Part of this negativity toward the Liberal Party is obviously an outgrowth of Mr. Zelaya's overthrow that was enabled by a revolt of the party's Congressional leadership, in partnership with the Supreme Court of Justice, the Armed Forces, and elements of the Nationalist Party. But another part was the result of a long-brewing dissatisfaction with the inability of the Liberal Party to noticeably improve the lives of the majority of Hondurans and successfully address the huge injustices within Honduran society. In the eyes of many Honduran Liberals, the differences between the Liberal Party and the Nationalist Party have grown to be insignificant. While there are clearly huge differences between the two philosophically, there is a strong perception that, in practice, there are none.

Logically, it is to the benefit of the Nationalist Party to do everything possible to fuel the fractionalization of the Liberal Party. Thus, when Mr. Lobo expresses support for the FNRP as a political party, it is not about giving legitimacy to or sympathizing with that movement... it is about weakening the Liberal Party to the point where it may not be able to win another presidential election anytime soon. Mr. Lobo's landslide win (56 percent) last November over Liberal Elvin Santos may well be the first in a long series of Nationalist Party victories and the beginning of the end of the Liberal Party's relevance in presidential elections... at least until the Liberals find a way to amicably settle their differences and unite.

The problem for the Liberal Party is that so long as Mr. Zelaya is around, true unity is nearly impossible. After all, mainstream Liberals probably feel a greater affinity toward their Nationalist brethren than to members of the FNRP. As long as Mr. Zelaya is seen as a leader and an icon of the FNRP, it is unlikely that the Liberal Party will be anywhere as strong as it once was in Honduras. In time, the FNRP may lose any sense of commonality with the Liberal Party, and this will only prolong the Liberal Party's absence from the Executive branch of government.

The idea of Honduras being dominated by one party should be of tremendous concern to all Hondurans. It is the competition between, at a minimum, two political parties that allows Honduras to call itself a democracy – albeit an imperfect one. Without a viable Liberal Party to promote liberal values, the Nationalist Party will be free to push a solidly conservative agenda that may be too narrow and oppressive for many people in Honduras. Each party has to have a credible counter-balance so that neither grows overly self-righteous, arrogant, and blind to the other sizeable part of the electorate that may not fare so well under its policies.

EPILOGUE

No matter how much evidence is presented to show that the overthrow of Manuel Zelaya as president was not a coup (or at least not a traditional coup), history will probably refer to it as such. Many people will think this is both extremely unfair and inaccurate. First impressions are often unfair and inaccurate, and yet they are often what remains with us and eventually become reality. Details and facts about events tend to become clouded because relatively few people are sufficiently interested or have an attention span long enough to understand exactly what occurred.

The lasting image that the world will have of the overthrow of President Zelaya will be of him being awakened by armed soldiers and flown out of Honduras in his pajamas. As the drama unfolded on television, radio, and the Internet, it appeared to the world that what was going on in Honduras was a coup because it looked like a coup. For better or worse, that will probably be the final judgment. The fact that the 192 member countries of the UN voted unanimously to condemn the "coup d'état in Honduras" will be the one fact that most people will repeatedly reference for years to come.

What may never be recognized, or may be easily forgotten, is that this "coup" was motivated by a desire to preserve democracy in Honduras. In that sense it could be called a "good coup". Honduras has been a chess piece in a larger geopolitical game being played by Hugo Chávez. While the perception in Honduras that Mr. Zelaya was attempting to change the Constitution in order to remain in power indefinitely created the environment that led to the overthrow, it was Mr. Chávez's interventionism and the fear that it generated within Honduran society that fueled the crisis. Mr. Zelaya has paid a high price for allowing himself to so willingly be manipulated by Mr. Chávez. Unfortunately, the people of Honduras have had to pay a huge price as well.

June 28, 2010 marked the one-year anniversary of Honduras' move to rid itself of Mr. Zelaya by force. The country is gradually recovering from this traumatic episode in its history. It has a new president in Porfirio Lobo and its relationship with the US is back to normal. US economic and military assistance is flowing once again. There is a Resistance movement, but its organization is relatively weak and it lacks a cause that can inspire and unify a majority of the Honduran people. There are still many countries in the Western Hemisphere that adamantly refuse to re-establish full diplomatic relations with Honduras until Mr. Zelaya is welcomed back to the country as some sort of national hero – something that is unlikely to occur.

Mr. Zelaya may remain for a time in his self-imposed exile in the Dominican Republic, where he can feel safe to make bold demands and unsubstantiated claims. He will continue to try and put his own spin on the events and players that caused his downfall. Mr. Zelaya may continue to make a lot of noise, but ultimately he will be more of an annoyance than anything else... both to Honduras and the US. In a letter addressed to thousands of his supporters who organized marches in Honduras to commemorate his ousting, Mr. Zelaya writes:

> "Everything indicates that the coup was planned at the [joint Honduran-US] military base in Palmerola by the US Southern Command and awkwardly executed by bad Hondurans. The causes and the masterminds of this crime that had previously been concealed are now clear, and what was suspected has now been confirmed: The United States was behind the coup d'état. The

intellectual authors of this crime answer to an illicit relationship between the hawks in Washington and Honduran business people and their subsidiaries – North Americans and financial institutions."

It must be acknowledged that for all his faults and missteps, Mr. Zelaya has given exposure to the plight of the vast majority of Hondurans who are poor and powerless, and thus lack the ability to significantly influence the manner in which their country is run. If Honduran society writes off Mr. Zelaya as an anomaly and opts to return to business as usual, rather than awakening from its apathy and mobilizing all of its human capital to resolve the inequities and injustices in Honduras, then it will condemn itself to the inevitable emergence of other Mels in the future... or worse.

ACKNOWLEDGEMENTS

I want to thank Stanley Marrder, the founder and publisher of *Honduras Weekly*, for allowing me wide latitude to express my opinions in his newspaper. Many thanks also to W. E. Gutman for his book publishing advice and words of encouragement.

My appreciation to Felipe Burchard for kindly allowing me to use the image of his wonderful painting "El Mago" (The Magician) for the front cover of this book.

I am indebted to my family for allowing me seemingly endless days on the computer. I am especially grateful to my wife for her invaluable editorial support, and for patiently listening to my ideas and providing thoughtful feedback.

* Half of all profits from the sales of this book will be donated to projecthonduras.com.

ABOUT THE AUTHOR

Marco Cáceres di Iorio is the editor of the online newspaper *Honduras Weekly*. He is also the cofounder of projecthonduras.com, an international network of volunteers involved in humanitarian development projects aimed at empowering the people of Honduras. He directs the annual Conference on Honduras in the town of Copán Ruinas in northwestern Honduras. He was born in Tegucigalpa.

www.ingramcontent.com/pod-product-compliance
Lightning Source LLC
Chambersburg PA
CBHW031503270326
41930CB00006B/223